favorite
simple meals

bring your family back to the table

favorite
simple meals
bring your family back to the table

Published by Publix Super Markets, Inc.
Copyright © 2007 by
Publix Super Markets, Inc.
P. O. Box 407
Lakeland, Florida 33802-0407
863.688.1188

Photography: Copyright © by Publix Super Markets, Inc.

Distributed in the United States by
Publix Super Markets, Inc.

Manufactured by **Favorite Recipes® Press**
An imprint of

FRP®

P. O. Box 305142
Nashville, Tennessee 37230
800.358.0560

Recipe for cover photograph appears on page 50.
Recipes for backcover photographs appear on pages 16, 112, and 144.

(more than) a few of our favorites
Though this collection of **favorite simple meals** recipes runs the gamut—from traditional dishes to exciting ethnic flavors—every selection has something in common: the resounding approval of our staff. We think you'll agree with us and find that these recipes are not only quick and easy to prepare, but decidedly delicious to eat.

skillet lasagna florentine
(recipe on page 28)

welcome to
apron's **favorite simple meals** cookbook

This Apron's cookbook continues our tradition of providing you with quick-and-easy meal ideas. Since publishing our original cookbook, the Apron's team has been busy developing hundreds of new recipes for you. For this cookbook, we've asked our staff to choose their favorites, bringing you the cream of the crop!

Our recipes are part of a program to help take meals from complex to comfortable. Using the ideas in this book, you can quickly prepare meals from the freshest ingredients. We have simplified planning, shopping, preparation, and cleanup in a number of ways. We use many convenience products to create our meals, which saves a lot of time in the kitchen. We provide a cooking sequence with each meal, which coordinates the steps in each recipe, to make preparing the meal complete and efficient. And cleanup is a snap because we try to reduce the number of cookware and utensils used. The result is delicious homecooked meals without the homecooked effort.

We hope you are already familiar with the Apron's program in most Publix locations. By rolling out the new Apron's meals centers over the last few years, we have upgraded more than just appliances. Our staff is now better equipped and eager to help you. We've installed multi-temperature display cases where all of the recipe ingredients are merchandised together. This allows you to quickly shop for dinner without searching the whole store for the ingredients you need. Our Apron's associates are also there to prepare the recipe while you observe, offer you a tasty sample, and answer any questions you have about the preparation or ingredients.

We have also included:

- A staples & standbys (pantry) section listing commonly used ingredients to help stock your kitchen, and
- A healthier options section that contains information about improving your dietary choices.

We feel confident you will enjoy our **favorite simple meals**. You can find even more of our recipes at www.publix.com/aprons. We hope this collection of recipes will make it easy to bring your family back to the table.

staples & standbys

PUBLIX®
Apron's
Simple Meals

Bring your family back to the table.

Today's featured meal.

- Children may sample, with parent's consent.

- Microwave in use.

- Samples may contain some of the following wholesome ingredients: peanuts, tree nuts, soybeans, wheat, fish, shellfish, milk and egg.

Everything in one place!

bring your family back to the table

This **favorite simple meals** cookbook is a continuation of our efforts to make your meal preparation easier and more convenient. One way to do this is to have a collection of staple ingredients on hand, and on standby, that are sure to help make cooking simple. These ingredients, organized by department, are used by our recipe development team to transform recipes from everyday to gourmet without taking a lot of extra time. We continually test new products to see what will save time, eliminate preparation, and make cleanup easy. Oh yes, and still improve the taste of your recipes. We also review products that may be less familiar, but will expand the flavors offered in our recipes, such as Hispanic seasonings, Asian sauces, and new spice and seasoning blends. These products work well in many of our meals and we feel sure that you may even decide to experiment with creating some new recipes of your own.

MEAT/SEAFOOD

fresh and frozen seafood

Publix carries a wide variety of fresh fish, shrimp, and shellfish. At the store, our Seafood associates are always glad to remove the skin and portion your fish for you. Our complete line of frozen seafood is easy to keep on hand in your freezer. With a few minutes to thaw, you can have dinner ready in just minutes. Unless noted otherwise, you can use fresh or thawed seafood in all of our recipes. We usually offer several varieties of fish that will work in each recipe.

chicken

Today there is a wide offering of chicken, more than just boneless, skinless chicken breasts. These cuts, often thinner, cook faster, save prep time, and are sure to get you to the table in less time. Other new products include those that are pre-seasoned to offer delicious flavor without having to buy extra spices and marinades.

You can also find a wide variety of fully cooked, seasoned chicken strips and pieces that can quickly pull the foundation of your meal together. Besides our recipes, your thoughts will start to take you to fast-and-easy meals to make on your own. From salads to soups and tortillas to skillet dinners, the possibilities are endless.

ready-to-cook and fully cooked meat

By customer request, you can now find a good selection of Ready-to-Cook meat and seafood entrees. Just pick out one that looks good, plan on a side recipe, along with a fresh salad, and you have a great meal without a lot of effort. Or check out the many pre-cooked selections that just need to be reheated before serving. Your family can experience a new flavor every night.

PRODUCE

bagged salads

It is hard to even remember how much trouble salads were before the bagged variety came along. Bagged salads are already washed and blended for convenience and unique flavors. Adding a salad also provides a fresh and nutritious balance to your meals. Since several different salad blends will work equally well in our recipes, when we call for fresh salad blend or romaine salad blend, feel free to substitute your favorite.

steak-topper and pre-diced vegetables

Fresh sliced vegetables do not have the shelf life of frozen, but they are hard to beat. Our steak-topper vegetables are a combination of fresh, pre-sliced mushrooms, onions, and bell peppers. Instead of taking time to clean, slice, and combine, you can pick up a great mix of flavors with all the work done for you.

While steak-topper vegetables used to be one of the few pre-sliced (or pre-diced) vegetable blends offered, today you will find many vegetables prepped and ready to go. Tomatoes, green bell peppers, zucchini and yellow squash, and many different types and colors of onions—just measure what you need. There is no chopping, no waste, and no tears.

herb and spice blend pastes

One of the best products that has come along recently is the selection of herbs and spices available in a paste form. The herbs and spices are picked in the height of the growing season to maximize their full taste, then chopped and packed into clear tubes to seal in the fresh flavor. They have the rich flavor, aroma, and nutrition of fresh herbs and spices without the time-consuming hassle of preparation. Available year round, they last up to three months in the refrigerator and six months in the freezer. Keeping them in the freezer extends their shelf life, yet they still remain pliable enough to use whenever needed. They come in many flavors including cilantro, basil, chili pepper blend, and ginger spice blend. Use the same amount as you would fresh chopped herbs or spices.

FROZEN

frozen diced onions, diced green peppers, and seasoning blend

Individually quick-frozen and pre-chopped vegetables are great time-saving ingredients. Keep any or all of these on hand for those times when you don't have fresh ingredients available. Just measure out what you need. Even when we call for fresh, you can use the frozen ones as a substitute.

DAIRY

butter

We have to face the facts. Fat adds flavor and we choose butter. Butter promotes browning, glazing, and provides a wonderful creamy texture. We also recommend butter because it has more flavor than margarine. Most of our recipes have been developed with salted butter, but you can use unsalted butter and adjust the seasoning to suit your family's preference. In addition, you will find garlic butter, which adds that special flavor with minimal effort. And, one of our favorites, herb garlic butter, makes fantastic garlic bread. Spread over sliced Bakery Italian bread and lightly toast. The flavor and herbs will really shine through.

refrigerated potatoes and pasta

Technology has brought us fresh potatoes that are peeled, cut, and ready to use. The varieties include: mashed potatoes, homestyle sliced, and red potato wedges, to name a few. Also, fresh refrigerated pasta cooks in less time than dried and often offers a wider variety of fillings and flavors.

cheese

You will find pre-sliced, shredded, crumbled, blended, and flavored cheese. Always have a selection on hand to change the ordinary to the extraordinary.

DRY GROCERY

nonstick foil and zip-top plastic bags

Nonstick foil is fantastic for making cleanup really easy. One place that it really shines is for lining your 2-sided tabletop grill. Start at the flow-through edge, then work your way toward the hinge side of the grill. Wrap the top cooking surface of the grill, too. Then preheat the grill. Cleaning is no longer a heavyweight match with you vs. the grill. Simply remove the foil and throw it away. You may even find that you use your grill more often when you learn this secret.

Zip-top bags make cleanup a snap and are called for in many of our recipes. We use zip-tops to coat, marinate, or blend ingredients. When you are finished, just toss the bag, along with the mess, into the trash.

pasta sauce

There are many great flavors of pasta sauce. We will make reference to the flavor used in each recipe. If desired, you can substitute your favorite brand or flavor. Some recipes will call for specialty pasta sauce. There are premium, gourmet pasta sauces that are really worth splurging on for the very best in flavor, quality, and seasoning. This category will also include ready-to-use Alfredo sauce, basil pesto, and sun-dried tomato pesto. If the recipe does not specify refrigerated, then you will find it on the pasta aisle. (Sun-dried tomato spread is found in the Produce department.)

dried pasta

Some of our recipes specifically call for multigrain pasta. If substituting regular pasta, you may need to adjust the amount of water or the cook time. You can also use multigrain pasta in place of regular by making similar adjustments.

seasonings

Some of the main seasonings that you find in our recipes are seasoned salt, seasoned pepper (or Montreal steak seasoning), and vegetable or meat seasoning blends. They are very versatile and add a nice blend of flavors from a single container. Some of the other seasonings that you will use include blackening seasoning (many types offered, but you can choose your favorite), Chinese five-spice powder, and several Hispanic seasonings such as Complete seasoning, adobo seasoning (a Spanish seasoned salt), and sazón with azafrán (a small packet used to add flavor).

red wine, white wine, marsala, and other wines

Sometimes what makes a recipe really taste distinctive is the flavor from a select wine. We have called for the type or variety that adds the best flavor. For best results, always use a wine that you would drink, instead of a cooking wine which has added salt. If you choose not to use wine, you may substitute an equal amount of an appropriate-flavored broth.

meaty mains

mediterranean
ribeye steaks
(recipe on page 18)

blackberry pork chops
(recipe on page 40)

hearty, flavorful, satisfying, and easy

Any of these recipe selections will let you thrill your hungry family in no time. With several comforting classics like country-fried steak and meatloaf, this section also includes some more novel flavor combinations, such as blackberry pork chops. But these are all simple meals to prepare. The only difficult part will be deciding which of them is your favorite.

shopping list

MEAT

1 1/2 lb grilling steaks
(such as top sirloin, ribeye,
or strip)

PRODUCE

11 fresh garlic cloves
8 ounces whole baby
   portabella mushrooms
1/4 cup pre-diced red onions

DAIRY

1/2 cup + 2 tablespoons
   butter
1 (4-ounce) container
   crumbled blue cheese

DRY GROCERY

3/4 teaspoon seasoned salt
1/4 cup soy sauce
1/2 teaspoon onion powder
1/2 teaspoon Montreal
   steak seasoning
1/2 teaspoon dried thyme
1/4 cup Marsala wine
cooking spray

SUGGESTED ITEMS

Caesar salad, sliced tomatoes,
   Key lime pie

savory steaks, garlic blue cheese butter, and marvelous mushrooms

MEAL TIME: *30 minutes*

COOKING SEQUENCE
• Prepare steaks and begin to marinate; preheat grill - 5 minutes
• Prepare butter and chill - 10 minutes
• Grill steaks; prepare mushrooms and serve - 15 minutes

SERVES: *4*

SHORTCUTS AND TIPS
To keep a steak from curling, cut several slits in the fat on the edge
of the steak.

UTENSILS AND COOKWARE

grill, grilling tongs   cooking spoons
large sauté pan with lid   meat thermometer
microwave-safe bowl   knife and cutting board
medium bowl, garlic press   measuring utensils

savory steaks

3 fresh garlic cloves

1/4 teaspoon seasoned salt

1/4 teaspoon pepper

1/4 cup soy sauce

1 1/2 lb grilling steaks (such as top sirloin, ribeye, or strip)

cooking spray

1. Crush garlic, using garlic press, into medium bowl. Use knife to remove garlic from bottom of press. Stir in seasoned salt, pepper, and soy sauce. Place steaks in marinade, turning to coat all sides (wash hands); marinate 10 minutes. Coat grill rack with cooking spray; then preheat on medium-high.

2. Place steaks on grill (wash hands); discard remaining marinade. Grill 5–8 minutes on each side or until internal temperature reaches 145°F (for medium-rare). Use a meat thermometer to accurately ensure desired doneness. (Grills vary widely; adjust time as needed.) Cut into portions, top with Garlic Blue Cheese Butter (recipe below) and serve.

CALORIES (per 1/4 recipe) 470kcal; FAT 32g; CHOL 115mg; SODIUM 1120mg; CARB 1g; FIBER 0g; PROTEIN 43g; VIT A 0%; VIT C 2%; CALC 6%; IRON 15%

garlic blue cheese butter

4 fresh garlic cloves

1/2 teaspoon onion powder

1/2 teaspoon Montreal steak seasoning

1/2 cup butter, divided

1 (4-ounce) container crumbled blue cheese (3/4 cup)

1/2 teaspoon dried thyme

1. Crush garlic, using garlic press, into microwave-safe bowl. Add onion powder, steak seasoning, and 2 tablespoons of the butter; microwave on HIGH 30 seconds or until butter melts.

2. Stir and microwave 1–2 more minutes, stirring once, or until hot and fragrant. Let sit to cool completely (about 5 minutes).

3. Cut remaining butter into small pieces; add to garlic mixture with blue cheese and thyme, mixing until well blended. Chill until ready to serve over Savory Steaks (recipe above) or fresh-baked Bakery bread. (Makes 8 servings.)

CALORIES (per 1/8 recipe) 150kcal; FAT 15g; CHOL 40mg; SODIUM 330mg; CARB 1g; FIBER 0g; PROTEIN 3g; VIT A 10%; VIT C 0%; CALC 8%; IRON 0%

marvelous mushrooms

2 tablespoons butter

1/4 cup pre-diced red onions

4 fresh garlic cloves

8 ounces whole baby portabella mushrooms (rinsed)

1/4 cup Marsala wine

1/2 teaspoon seasoned salt

1. Preheat large sauté on medium-high 2–3 minutes.

2. Add butter and onions to pan. Crush garlic, using garlic press, into pan. Cook 1–2 minutes or until browned.

3. Stir in remaining ingredients. Reduce heat to medium; cover and cook 5 minutes, stirring occasionally. Serve.

CALORIES (per 1/4 recipe) 100kcal; FAT 6g; CHOL 15mg; SODIUM 240mg; CARB 7g; FIBER 1g; PROTEIN 3g; VIT A 4%; VIT C 4%; CALC 2%; IRON 2%

Everyone has their own favorite steak for grilling. You can find nice thick steaks for grilling, from about 1-inch-thick to about 1 1/2-inches-thick. The thicker steaks will take a little longer to cook, but the flavor and juiciness will be worth it. ALWAYS use a meat thermometer to accurately check for the desired doneness. Lift the steak off the grill and insert the thermometer sideways into the steak; make sure the notched sensing portion is fully inserted.

shopping list

MEAT

1 1/2 lb grilling ribeye steaks
(or top sirloin or strip)

PRODUCE

1 bag fresh baby spinach
leaves (5–6 oz)
1/4 cup pre-diced red onions
2 tablespoons pine nuts

FROZEN

1 (16.9-ounce) package
potato/cheese pierogies

DAIRY

2 tablespoons butter
1/4 cup crumbled feta cheese
1 tablespoon shredded
Parmesan cheese

DRY GROCERY

1/4 cup Italian bread crumbs
2 tablespoons sun-dried
tomato pesto
1 1/2 cups specialty vodka
pasta sauce

SUGGESTED ITEMS

fresh salad blend, garlic
bread, cheesecake

mediterranean ribeye steaks with pierogies à la vodka

MEAL TIME: *25 minutes*

COOKING SEQUENCE
- Prepare steaks through step 1 - 5 minutes
- Prepare pierogies and begin to bring to boil - 10 minutes
- Complete steaks; complete pierogies and serve - 10 minutes

SERVES: *4*

SHORTCUTS AND TIPS

Want to grill instead? Grill ribeyes until close to desired doneness. Prepare feta topping and add to top of steaks during last few minutes of grill time. (Grills vary widely; adjust time as needed.)

UTENSILS AND COOKWARE

large sauté pan
medium saucepan with lid
microwave-safe bowl with lid
spatula, tongs, cooking spoons

meat thermometer
knife and cutting board
measuring utensils

mediterranean ribeye steaks

1 bag fresh baby spinach leaves (5–6 oz)

1 1/2 lb grilling ribeye steaks (or top sirloin or strip)

1/4 teaspoon salt

1/8 teaspoon pepper

1 tablespoon butter

1/4 cup pre-diced red onions

1/4 cup crumbled feta cheese

1/4 cup Italian bread crumbs

2 tablespoons sun-dried tomato pesto

1. Chop spinach coarsely and place in microwave-safe bowl. Cover and microwave on HIGH 2–3 minutes or until tender. Drain thoroughly.

2. Preheat large sauté pan on medium 2–3 minutes. Cut steaks into 4 portions; sprinkle both sides with salt and pepper (wash hands).

3. Place butter in pan; swirl to coat. Add steaks (wash hands) and onions; cook 5–8 minutes on each side or until internal temperature reaches 145°F (for medium-rare). Use a meat thermometer to accurately ensure desired doneness.

4. Meanwhile, stir feta cheese, bread crumbs, and tomato pesto into spinach, mixing thoroughly. During last two minutes of steak cook time, spread 1/4 cup spinach mixture over top of steaks. Carefully turn steaks and spinach mixture over to heat topping; cook 1–2 more minutes or until golden and slightly crusty. Gently turn steaks over and serve.

NOTE: *This topping may also be browned, using an oven broiler.*

CALORIES (per 1/4 recipe) 370kcal; FAT 20g; CHOL 115mg; SODIUM 580mg; CARB 8g; FIBER 1g; PROTEIN 38g; VIT A 45%; VIT C 10%; CALC 10%; IRON 25%

pierogies à la vodka

1 (16.9-ounce) package frozen potato/cheese pierogies

1 cup water

1 tablespoon butter

1 1/2 cups specialty vodka pasta sauce

2 tablespoons pine nuts

1 tablespoon shredded Parmesan cheese

1. Place pierogies, water, and butter in medium saucepan; cover and bring to boil on medium-high. Boil 2–3 minutes, stirring occasionally.

2. Remove lid; boil 1–2 more minutes, stirring often, or until most of liquid is absorbed.

3. Gently stir in pasta sauce; reduce heat to medium. Cook 3–4 minutes, stirring occasionally, or until sauce is thoroughly heated and begins to thicken. Stir in pine nuts; sprinkle with cheese before serving.

CALORIES (per 1/4 recipe) 387kcal; FAT 22g; CHOL 46mg; SODIUM 973mg; CARB 39g; FIBER 3g; PROTEIN 9g; VIT A 25%; VIT C 32%; CALC 7%; IRON 17%

When purchasing packaged salad greens make sure the package is cold to the touch and the colors of the greens are bright. The package should not include any brown-tipped or bruised greens. Pay close attention to the expiration date printed on the package.

shopping list

MEAT

1 1/2 lb grilling top sirloin
   steaks (or ribeye or strip)

PRODUCE

1 medium zucchini
1 small red onion
6 large white mushroom caps
1 small yellow bell pepper
10–12 sprigs fresh thyme

DAIRY

1 (24-ounce) package
   refrigerated mashed
   potatoes
3 tablespoons crumbled
   blue cheese
1 tablespoon butter

DRY GROCERY

1/4 cup extra-virgin olive oil
3/4 teaspoon Montreal
   steak seasoning
2 teaspoons Buffalo
   wing sauce

SUGGESTED ITEMS

sourdough bread,
   chocolate cake

sirloin steaks and vegetables with buffalo mashed potatoes

MEAL TIME: *35 minutes*

COOKING SEQUENCE

- Preheat grill
- Prepare steaks and vegetables; complete grilling - 20 minutes
- While steaks stand, prepare potatoes - 5 minutes
- Cut vegetables and slice steaks; serve - 10 minutes

SERVES: *4*

SHORTCUTS AND TIPS

For best results, cook steaks initially on hottest part of grill to
mark outsides. Move steaks to slower side of grill to finish cooking,
for tenderness.

UTENSILS AND COOKWARE

grill, grilling tongs   meat thermometer
microwave-safe bowl with lid   knife and cutting board
large bowl, cooking spoons   measuring utensils

sirloin steaks and vegetables

1 medium zucchini

1 small red onion

6 large white mushroom caps

1 small yellow bell pepper

1/4 cup extra-virgin olive oil, divided

1/2 teaspoon salt

1/8 teaspoon pepper

1 1/2 lb grilling top sirloin steaks (or ribeye or strip)

3/4 teaspoon Montreal steak seasoning

10–12 sprigs fresh thyme (rinsed)

1. Preheat grill on medium-high. Rinse all vegetables; remove ends, peel, and seeds, as needed. Cut vegetables into halves or quarters. (If using outdoor grill, larger pieces are easier to manage while grilling. If using tabletop grill, cut into 2-inch chunks.) Place in large bowl; add 2 tablespoons of the olive oil, salt, and pepper. Toss or stir until evenly coated.

2. Sprinkle both sides of steaks with steak seasoning and place on grill (wash hands); add vegetables. Close lid (or cover loosely with foil); grill steaks 5–8 minutes on each side or until internal temperature reaches 145°F (for medium-rare). Use a meat thermometer to accurately ensure desired doneness. Meanwhile, turn vegetables occasionally and cook until crisp-tender or desired tenderness. Cook time may be slightly more or less than for steaks. (Grills vary widely; adjust time as needed.)

3. Cut vegetables, if desired, and place on serving platter. Chop thyme leaves finely (1 tablespoon); sprinkle over vegetables. Drizzle with remaining 2 tablespoons olive oil. Cut steak diagonally into thin slices and arrange over vegetables. Serve.

CALORIES (per 1/4 recipe) 510kcal; FAT 38g; CHOL 90mg; SODIUM 510mg; CARB 6g; FIBER 2g; PROTEIN 37g; VIT A 4%; VIT C 60%; CALC 6%; IRON 20%

buffalo mashed potatoes

1 (24-ounce) package refrigerated mashed potatoes

3 tablespoons crumbled blue cheese, divided

1 tablespoon butter

2 teaspoons Buffalo wing sauce

1. Combine all ingredients (except 1 tablespoon of the blue cheese) in microwave-safe bowl.

2. Cover and microwave on HIGH 2 minutes. Stir and heat 2–3 more minutes or until hot. Sprinkle with remaining blue cheese. Serve.

CALORIES (per 1/4 recipe) 250kcal; FAT 17g; CHOL 35mg; SODIUM 810mg; CARB 21g; FIBER 1g; PROTEIN 4g; VIT A 15%; VIT C 2%; CALC 8%; IRON 2%

When using tongs to handle and turn raw meat, always use a second (clean) pair to transfer the cooked meat off the grill. This reduces the potential for any cross-contamination problems. Your serving platter should also be clean; one that has not been in contact with raw meat.

shopping list

MEAT

1 1/2 lb grilling steaks
(such as top sirloin, ribeye,
or strip)

PRODUCE

8 fresh garlic cloves
1 head iceberg lettuce
1 cucumber
1 red bell pepper
1 pint grape tomatoes
8 ounces whole baby
portabella mushrooms

DAIRY

1/3 cup butter
1 (20-ounce) package
refrigerated red
potato wedges

DRY GROCERY

1/4 cup extra-virgin olive oil
1 teaspoon Montreal
steak seasoning
aluminum foil
1 packet onion soup mix
(about 1 ounce)
1/2 cup ranch salad dressing

SUGGESTED ITEMS

yeast rolls, cheesecake

garlic steak with mushrooms, onion-roasted potatoes, wedge salad

MEAL TIME: *40 minutes*

COOKING SEQUENCE

- Preheat oven; prepare steak and begin to marinate - 5 minutes
- Prepare potatoes and begin to bake - 10 minutes
- Begin to cook steak; prepare salad (using clean knife and cutting board) and serve - 25 minutes

SERVES: *4*

SHORTCUTS AND TIPS

If grilling steak, marinate 30–40 minutes for more flavor.

UTENSILS AND COOKWARE

large sauté pan with lid
baking sheet, serving platter
2 medium bowls
garlic press, tongs

cooking spoons
meat thermometer
knife and cutting board
measuring utensils

garlic steak with mushrooms

8 fresh garlic cloves

2 tablespoons extra-virgin olive oil

1 teaspoon Montreal steak seasoning

1/2 teaspoon salt

1 1/2 lb grilling steaks (such as top sirloin, ribeye, or strip)

1/3 cup butter

8 ounces whole baby portabella mushrooms (rinsed)

1. Crush garlic, using garlic press, into medium bowl. Use knife to remove garlic from bottom of press. Stir in olive oil, steak seasoning, and salt. Cut steak into four portions; add to garlic mixture. Press mixture into steaks and turn to coat completely (wash hands). Let stand 10 minutes.

2. Preheat large sauté pan on medium-high 2–3 minutes. Place steaks and garlic mixture in pan (wash hands); cook 5 minutes (do not turn). Reduce heat to medium; turn steaks and cook 6–8 more minutes or until internal temperature is 145°F (for medium-rare). Use a meat thermometer to accurately ensure desired doneness; adjust time as needed.

3. Add butter and turn steaks to coat. Remove steaks and cover to keep warm. Add mushrooms to pan; cover and cook 5–7 minutes or until tender. Serve with steaks.

CALORIES (per 1/4 recipe) 580kcal; FAT 46g; CHOL 130mg; SODIUM 670mg; CARB 4g; FIBER 0g; PROTEIN 36g; VIT A 10%; VIT C 4%; CALC 6%; IRON 15%

onion-roasted potatoes

aluminum foil

2 tablespoons extra-virgin olive oil

1 (20-ounce) package refrigerated red potato wedges

1 packet onion soup mix (about 1 ounce)

1. Preheat oven to 400°F. Line baking sheet with foil (for easy cleanup).

2. Combine all ingredients in medium bowl; spread in single layer on baking sheet. Bake 10 minutes.

3. Turn potatoes; bake 15–20 more minutes or until potatoes are tender when pierced with a fork. Serve.

CALORIES (per 1/4 recipe) 170kcal; FAT 7g; CHOL 0mg; SODIUM 1050mg; CARB 22g; FIBER 4g; PROTEIN 4g; VIT A 0%; VIT C 8%; CALC 2%; IRON 4%

wedge salad

1 head iceberg lettuce

1 red bell pepper

1 cucumber

1 pint grape tomatoes

1/2 cup ranch salad dressing

1. Rinse all vegetables; remove outer lettuce leaves and trim core. Place lettuce on cutting board with core end up. Cut in half through core, then slice each half again (makes 4 wedges); arrange on serving platter.

2. Cut pepper into rings (remove seeds) and cucumber into bite-size pieces. Arrange vegetables around wedges; serve with dressing.

CALORIES (per 1/4 recipe) 180kcal; FAT 14g; CHOL 10mg; SODIUM 270mg; CARB 13g; FIBER 4g; PROTEIN 3g; VIT A 50%; VIT C 130%; CALC 4%; IRON 8%

shopping list

MEAT

4 beef cube steaks
(about 1 1/2 lb)

PRODUCE

1 (12-ounce) bag snipped
green beans

DAIRY

2 tablespoons butter
1 (24-ounce) package
refrigerated mashed
potatoes
1/4 cup milk
2 large eggs (or 1/2 cup
egg substitute)

DRY GROCERY

1 teaspoon seasoned salt
1/4 cup flour
2/3 cup plain bread crumbs
3 tablespoons canola oil
1 packet sausage gravy mix
(about 2.5 ounce)
1 (12-ounce) can
evaporated milk
1 tablespoon cooked
bacon pieces

SUGGESTED ITEMS

biscuits, apple pie

country-fried steak, peppered mashed potatoes, and southern green beans

MEAL TIME: *30 minutes*

COOKING SEQUENCE

- Prepare potatoes through step 1 and beans through step 1 - 5 minutes
- Prepare steaks and begin to cook - 10 minutes
- Complete beans - 10 minutes
- Complete steaks and potatoes; serve - 5 minutes

SERVES: *4*

SHORTCUTS AND TIPS

To reduce fat content by about 30%, try the steak recipe with chicken cutlets and reduce the canola oil to 2 tablespoons.

UTENSILS AND COOKWARE

large sauté pan
medium saucepan with lid
microwave-safe bowl with lid

mixing bowls, colander
tongs, cooking spoons
measuring utensils

country-fried steak

1/4 cup flour

1/2 teaspoon seasoned salt

2 large eggs, beaten
(or 1/2 cup egg substitute)

2/3 cup plain bread crumbs

4 beef cube steaks
(about 1 1/2 lb)

3 tablespoons canola oil

1 packet sausage gravy mix
(about 2.5 ounce)

1 (12-ounce) can evaporated milk

1 cup water

1. Combine flour and seasoned salt in medium bowl. Place eggs in second bowl and bread crumbs in third bowl. Preheat large sauté pan on medium 1–2 minutes. Dredge each steak in flour mixture, coating evenly. Dip into eggs; remove and let excess drip off. Dredge in bread crumbs (wash hands).
2. Place oil in pan; swirl to coat. Add steaks (wash hands); cook 3–4 minutes on each side or until golden. Remove from pan and cover to keep warm.
3. Stir in gravy mix and gradually add milk and water, stirring continuously, until gravy is smooth. Reduce heat to low and cook 2–3 minutes, stirring often, to heat thoroughly. Serve gravy over steaks.

CALORIES (per 1/4 recipe) 680kcal; FAT 37g; CHOL 225mg; SODIUM 1170mg; CARB 36g; FIBER 1g; PROTEIN 47g; VIT A 6%; VIT C 2%; CALC 30%; IRON 30%

peppered mashed potatoes

1 (24-ounce) package refrigerated mashed potatoes

1/4 cup milk

1 tablespoon butter

1 1/2 teaspoons pepper

1. Combine all ingredients in microwave-safe bowl; cover.
2. Microwave on HIGH 4 minutes, stirring once, or until hot. Stir and serve.

CALORIES (per 1/4 recipe) 240kcal; FAT 15g; CHOL 35mg; SODIUM 660mg; CARB 22g; FIBER 1g; PROTEIN 3g; VIT A 10%; VIT C 0%; CALC 6%; IRON 4%

southern green beans

1 (12-ounce) bag snipped green beans (rinsed)

2 cups water

1 tablespoon cooked bacon pieces

1 tablespoon butter

1/2 teaspoon seasoned salt

1/8 teaspoon pepper

1. Place beans and water in medium saucepan on high and bring to boil. Boil 7 minutes, stirring occasionally, or until beans begin to soften.
2. Drain; stir in remaining ingredients. Cover, reduce heat to low, and cook 8–10 minutes, stirring occasionally, or until desired tenderness. Serve.

CALORIES (per 1/4 recipe) 60kcal; FAT 3.5g; CHOL 10mg; SODIUM 250mg; CARB 6g; FIBER 3g; PROTEIN 2g; VIT A 15%; VIT C 25%; CALC 4%; IRON 6%

shopping list

MEAT

1 lb lean ground beef, 7% fat

FROZEN

1 cup seasoning blend (diced
  onions, bell peppers, celery)
1 (16-ounce) bag green beans

DAIRY

1 cup reduced-fat milk
2 eggs (or 1/2 cup
  egg substitute)
2 tablespoons garlic butter

DRY GROCERY

20 reduced-fat
  buttery-taste crackers
large zip-top bag
1 teaspoon meat
  seasoning blend
cooking spray
1/4 cup ketchup
1/4 cup maple syrup
1 (4.9-ounce) box au gratin
  potato mix
1 teaspoon seasoned salt
1 (14.5-ounce) can diced
  Italian-style tomatoes

SUGGESTED ITEMS

applesauce, dinner rolls,
  cherry pie

mom's meatloaf, creamy potatoes, and italian green beans

MEAL TIME: *55 minutes*

COOKING SEQUENCE
- Prepare meatloaf and begin to bake - 10 minutes
- 10 minutes into bake time, prepare potatoes through step 2 - 35 minutes
- Complete meatloaf and potatoes, prepare beans, and serve - 10 minutes

SERVES: *4*

SHORTCUTS AND TIPS

Use residual heat in the oven to warm your cherry pie. Just remove the
plastic cover, pop the pie in oven, and it will be toasty warm when you
finish your meal.

UTENSILS AND COOKWARE

9 × 4-inch loaf pan
medium saucepan with lid
microwave-safe bowl with lid
mixing bowls

cooking spoons
meat thermometer
measuring utensils

mom's meatloaf

cooking spray

20 reduced-fat buttery-taste crackers

large zip-top bag

1 lb lean ground beef, 7% fat

1 cup frozen seasoning blend (diced onions, bell peppers, celery)

1/2 cup reduced-fat milk

2 eggs (or 1/2 cup egg substitute)

1 teaspoon meat seasoning blend

1/4 teaspoon salt

1/8 teaspoon pepper

1/4 cup ketchup

1/4 cup maple syrup

1. Preheat oven to 375°F. Coat 9 × 4-inch loaf pan with cooking spray.

2. Place crackers in zip-top bag and crush finely. Combine all ingredients (except ketchup and syrup) in medium bowl, mixing just until combined (do not over-mix). Place in pan and shape into a loaf (wash hands). Bake 40–45 minutes or until internal temperature reaches 165°F or higher. Use a meat thermometer to accurately ensure doneness.

3. Combine ketchup and syrup in small bowl. Five minutes before bake time is complete, pour over meatloaf; complete bake time. Let stand 5 minutes before serving.

CALORIES (per 1/4 recipe) 368kcal; FAT 13g; CHOL 175mg; SODIUM 714mg; CARB 32g; FIBER <1g; PROTEIN 28g; VIT A 7%; VIT C 4%; CALC 8%; IRON 24%

creamy potatoes

2 cups water

1/2 cup reduced-fat milk

2 tablespoons garlic butter

1 (4.9-ounce) box au gratin potato mix

1/4 teaspoon salt

1/8 teaspoon pepper

1. Place water, milk, and garlic butter in medium saucepan. Bring to boil on high.

2. Stir potatoes, seasoning (from flavor packet), salt, and pepper into boiling water. Cover and reduce heat to medium-low; cook 20 minutes, stirring occasionally, or until potatoes are tender.

3. Remove from heat; let stand 5 minutes. Serve.

CALORIES (per 1/4 recipe) 190kcal; FAT 8g; CHOL 15mg; SODIUM 1050mg; CARB 27g; FIBER 2g; PROTEIN 4g; VIT A 6%; VIT C 10%; CALC 10%; IRON 2%

italian green beans

1 (16-ounce) bag frozen green beans

1 (14.5-ounce) can diced Italian-style tomatoes

1 teaspoon seasoned salt

1. Combine all ingredients in microwave-safe bowl.

2. Cover and microwave on HIGH 10 minutes, stirring once. Stir and serve.

CALORIES (per 1/4 recipe) 80kcal; FAT 0g; CHOL 0mg; SODIUM 780mg; CARB 17g; FIBER 4g; PROTEIN 3g; VIT A 15%; VIT C 45%; CALC 10%; IRON 8%

shopping list

MEAT

1 lb lean ground beef, 7% fat

PRODUCE

4 ounces pre-sliced baby portabella mushrooms
1/3 cup pre-diced onions
1/3 cup pre-diced green bell peppers
1 bag fresh baby spinach leaves (5–6 oz)
1 bag romaine salad blend (8–10 oz)
1 cup grape tomatoes

DAIRY

1 3/4 cups shredded Italian-blend cheese
1/4 cup crumbled Gorgonzola cheese

DRY GROCERY

1 (26-ounce) jar onion/garlic pasta sauce
1 (9-ounce) box no-boil lasagna pasta
1/2 cup seasoned croutons
1/4 cup ranch salad dressing with bacon

SUGGESTED ITEMS

garlic bread, layer cake

skillet lasagna florentine with simple salad

MEAL TIME: *30 minutes*

COOKING SEQUENCE
- Prepare lasagna and begin final cook time - 15 minutes
- Prepare salad and serve - 15 minutes

SERVES: *4*

SHORTCUTS AND TIPS
Spice things up by using mild Italian sausage in the lasagna instead of ground beef.

UTENSILS AND COOKWARE
large skillet (or sauté pan) with lid
microwave-safe bowl with lid
salad bowl, tongs

cooking spoon
measuring utensils

skillet lasagna florentine

1 lb lean ground beef, 7% fat

4 ounces pre-sliced baby portabella mushrooms (rinsed)

1/3 cup pre-diced onions

1/3 cup pre-diced green bell peppers

1 (26-ounce) jar onion/garlic pasta sauce

1 cup water

1 (9-ounce) box no-boil lasagna pasta

1 bag fresh baby spinach leaves (5–6 oz)

1 3/4 cups shredded Italian-blend cheese

1. Crumble ground beef into microwave-safe bowl (wash hands). Stir in mushrooms, onions, and peppers. Cover and microwave on HIGH 8 minutes, stirring once, or until most of meat is cooked. Stir in pasta sauce and water until well blended.

2. Spread 2 1/2 cups of the meat sauce in bottom of large skillet. Then build layers: 4 noodles, spread with 1 cup of the meat sauce, arrange 1 cup of the spinach leaves over sauce, and sprinkle 1/4 cup of the cheese over spinach. Repeat layer two more times. Add remaining 4 noodles; top with remaining meat sauce. Sprinkle with remaining cheese.

3. Cover and cook 3–4 minutes on medium-high or until sauce begins to boil. Reduce heat to medium; cook 10 minutes or until pasta is tender, most of liquid is absorbed, and cheese melts. Serve. (Makes 6 servings.)

CALORIES (per 1/6 recipe) 490kcal; FAT 17g; CHOL 65mg; SODIUM 790mg; CARB 53g; FIBER 4g; PROTEIN 32g; VIT A 30%; VIT C 25%; CALC 30%; IRON 20%

simple salad

1 bag romaine salad blend (8–10 oz)

1 cup grape tomatoes (rinsed)

1/2 cup seasoned croutons

1/4 cup crumbled Gorgonzola cheese

1/4 cup ranch salad dressing with bacon

1. Place salad blend, tomatoes, and croutons in salad bowl.

2. Add remaining ingredients; toss and serve.

CALORIES (per 1/4 recipe) 150kcal; FAT 11g; CHOL 10mg; SODIUM 290mg; CARB 9g; FIBER 2g; PROTEIN 4g; VIT A 25%; VIT C 30%; CALC 6%; IRON 4%

When baking or cooking, place a clear glass baking dish over your open cookbook to hold the book open and to keep it clean. You will be able to read the recipe clearly through the glass.

shopping list

MEAT

1 package fully cooked beef
pot roast (about 1 lb)

PRODUCE

3/4 cup pre-diced red onions
8 ounces pre-sliced baby
portabella mushrooms
2 teaspoons minced garlic

FROZEN

1 (14-ounce) bag
broccoli florets

DAIRY

1 tablespoon butter
1/4 cup sour cream
1/4 ounce Asiago cheese

DRY GROCERY

8 ounces extra-wide egg
noodles
1/4 cup roasted red peppers
2 tablespoons extra-virgin
olive oil

SUGGESTED ITEMS

biscuits, favorite fruit pie

pot roast stroganoff with sicilian broccoli

MEAL TIME: *25 minutes*

COOKING SEQUENCE

- Prepare stroganoff through step 2 - 5 minutes
- Prepare broccoli through step 3 - 10 minutes
- Complete stroganoff and broccoli; serve - 10 minutes

SERVES: *4*

SHORTCUTS AND TIPS

The portabella mushrooms add a rich mushroom flavor to this easy
"comfort" meal.

UTENSILS AND COOKWARE

large sauté pan with lid
medium saucepan with lid
colander, cheese grater

cooking spoons
knife and cutting board
measuring utensils

pot roast stroganoff

1 tablespoon butter

1/4 cup pre-diced red onions

8 ounces pre-sliced baby portabella mushrooms (rinsed)

2 cups water

8 ounces extra-wide egg noodles

1/4 cup roasted red peppers

1 package fully cooked beef pot roast (about 1 lb)

1/4 cup sour cream

1/8 teaspoon pepper

1. Place butter, onions, mushrooms, water, and noodles in large sauté pan; cover and bring to boil on medium-high.

2. Remove cover when mixture begins to boil. Boil 5–6 minutes, stirring occasionally, or until most of liquid is absorbed. Meanwhile, cut red peppers into thin strips.

3. Remove pot roast from packaging (reserve gravy). Cut meat into bite-size pieces. Stir pot roast, reserved gravy, red peppers, and sour cream into noodle mixture; cook 2–3 minutes (uncovered), stirring often, or until thoroughly heated. Season with pepper and serve.

CALORIES (per 1/4 recipe) 490kcal; FAT 20g; CHOL 140mg; SODIUM 510mg; CARB 48g; FIBER 3g; PROTEIN 31g; VIT A 20%; VIT C 20%; CALC 4%; IRON 25%

sicilian broccoli

1 (14-ounce) bag frozen broccoli florets

2 tablespoons extra-virgin olive oil

1/2 cup pre-diced red onions

2 teaspoons minced garlic

1/2 teaspoon salt

1/8 teaspoon pepper

1/4 ounce Asiago cheese

1. Fill medium saucepan half full of water. Cover and bring to a boil on high for broccoli.

2. Stir broccoli into boiling water. Boil 3–4 minutes, stirring occasionally, or until desired tenderness. Drain broccoli thoroughly.

3. Return saucepan to stove; reduce to medium-high. Place olive oil in pan; swirl to coat. Add onions and garlic; cook 2–3 minutes to brown.

4. Stir in broccoli until coated with oil. Cook 3–4 more minutes, stirring occasionally, or until flavors are well blended. Season with salt and pepper; grate cheese (about 1 tablespoon) over broccoli and serve.

CALORIES (per 1/4 recipe) 110kcal; FAT 8g; CHOL 0mg; SODIUM 330mg; CARB 8g; FIBER 3g; PROTEIN 4g; VIT A 25%; VIT C 120%; CALC 6%; IRON 4%

We take a fully cooked meat product and enhance it a bit to create a great homestyle meal that doesn't require all-day-cooking effort.

shopping list

MEAT

4 slices smoked bacon
2 pork tenderloins
(about 2 lb)

PRODUCE

1 1/2 cups tart apple slices
6–7 fresh sage leaves
1 (3-lb) bag small
red potatoes
1/2 ounce fresh Italian parsley

DAIRY

1/4 cup butter (1/2 stick)

DRY GROCERY

1 cup chicken broth
2 tablespoons light
brown sugar
1/4 cup red wine vinegar
1 tablespoon + 1 teaspoon
seasoned salt

SUGGESTED ITEMS

fresh asparagus, rye bread,
crumb cake

apple sage pork with parsley red potatoes

MEAL TIME: *35 minutes*

COOKING SEQUENCE

- Prepare potatoes and begin to boil - 10 minutes
- Prepare pork - 10 minutes
- Complete potatoes and pork; serve - 15 minutes

SERVES: 6

SHORTCUTS AND TIPS

If you have extra fresh herbs on hand, arrange in a vase with fresh flowers for an aromatic herb bouquet.

UTENSILS AND COOKWARE

large saucepan with lid
large sauté pan with lid
colander, tongs
cooking spoons

meat thermometer
knife and cutting board
measuring utensils

apple sage pork

4 slices smoked bacon

2 pork tenderloins (about 2 lb)

1 teaspoon seasoned salt

1/4 teaspoon pepper

1 1/2 cups tart apple slices

6–7 fresh sage leaves (rinsed)

1 cup chicken broth

2 tablespoons light brown sugar

2 tablespoons red wine vinegar

1. Cut bacon into 1/4-inch pieces and place in large sauté pan. Cook on medium-high 1–2 minutes. Sprinkle pork tenderloin with seasoned salt and pepper (wash hands and cutting board with hot soapy water).

2. Place pork in pan (wash hands); cover and cook 6–8 minutes, turning pork and stirring bacon occasionally, or until browned. Cut apple slices into bite-sized pieces. Chop sage leaves finely (1 tablespoon).

3. Stir in apples, sage, and remaining ingredients; bring to a boil. Reduce heat to medium; cook (uncovered) 12–15 minutes, turning and stirring occasionally, or until sauce has reduced by half and internal temperature of pork reaches 160°F (for medium). Use a meat thermometer to accurately ensure doneness. Slice pork and serve with apple sage sauce.

CALORIES (per 1/6 recipe) 280kcal; FAT 12g; CHOL 100mg; SODIUM 600mg; CARB 7g; FIBER 1g; PROTEIN 34g; VIT A 0%; VIT C 4%; CALC 2%; IRON 10%

parsley red potatoes

1 (3-lb) bag small red potatoes (rinsed)

2 tablespoons red wine vinegar

1 tablespoon seasoned salt

1/2 teaspoon pepper

1/2 ounce fresh Italian parsley (rinsed)

1/4 cup butter (1/2 stick)

1. Fill large saucepan 1/2 full of water. Bring to a boil on high. Meanwhile, cut potatoes in half and add to water. Stir in vinegar, seasoned salt, and pepper. Boil 12–14 minutes or until potatoes are tender.

2. Chop parsley leaves finely, then measure (1/4 cup). Drain potatoes and return to pan. Stir in parsley and butter. Cover and let stand until ready to serve.

CALORIES (per 1/6 recipe) 253kcal; FAT 8g; CHOL 21mg; SODIUM 847mg; CARB 42g; FIBER 3g; PROTEIN 5g; VIT A 3%; VIT C 70%; CALC 4%; IRON 11%

To keep parsley fresh, rinse and shake off the excess moisture. Wrap in several thicknesses of paper towels and store in a zip-top bag in the refrigerator.

shopping list

MEAT
2 pork tenderloins
(about 2 lb)

PRODUCE
1 cup sweet Vidalia
onions/peppers relish

FROZEN
2 cups sliced peaches
1 (9-ounce) box cut
green beans

DAIRY
1 (20-ounce) package
refrigerated red
potato wedges
3 tablespoons garlic butter

DRY GROCERY
1/2 cup pecan pieces
1/2 cup French-fried onions
1 tablespoon + 2 teaspoons
light brown sugar
olive oil cooking spray
2 tablespoons dried parsley

SUGGESTED ITEMS
sliced tomatoes, biscuits,
pecan pie

pecan-roasted pork, georgia chutney, and green beans and potatoes

MEAL TIME: *45 minutes*

COOKING SEQUENCE
- Start water for beans; prepare pork and begin to bake - 15 minutes
- Prepare chutney (use clean knife and cutting board); begin final cook time - 5 minutes
- Complete beans and pork; serve - 25 minutes

SERVES: 6

SHORTCUTS AND TIPS
Did you know Vidalia onions are grown in twenty Georgia counties? Only onions grown in those counties can truly be called Vidalia.

UTENSILS AND COOKWARE
large saucepan with lid
medium saucepan with lid
food processor
baking sheet, colander

cooking spoons
meat thermometer
knife and cutting board
measuring utensils

pecan-roasted pork

olive oil cooking spray
1/2 cup pecan pieces
1/2 cup French-fried onions
1 tablespoon light brown sugar
2 pork tenderloins (about 2 lb)
1/2 teaspoon salt
1/8 teaspoon pepper

1. Preheat oven to 425°F. Coat baking sheet with cooking spray. Place pecans, onions, and sugar in food processor and process until coarsely chopped; place mixture on plate (may be paper).
2. Season pork with salt and pepper; roll in pecan mixture until well coated and place 1 inch apart on baking sheet. Coat top of tenderloins with cooking spray (wash hands and cutting board). Bake 25–30 minutes or until internal temperature reaches 160°F (for medium). Use a meat thermometer to accurately ensure doneness.
3. Let pork stand 5 minutes; then cut into 1-inch-thick slices. Top with Georgia Chutney (recipe below) and serve.

CALORIES (per 1/6 recipe) 280kcal; FAT 15g; CHOL 100mg; SODIUM 300mg; CARB 5g; FIBER 1g; PROTEIN 33g; VIT A 0%; VIT C 2%; CALC 2%; IRON 10%

georgia chutney

2 cups frozen sliced peaches
1 cup sweet Vidalia onions/peppers relish
2 teaspoons light brown sugar

1. Cut peaches into bite-size pieces; combine with remaining ingredients in medium saucepan.
2. Cover and bring to a boil on medium-low; cook 20–25 minutes, stirring occasionally, or until thickened. Serve over pork slices.

CALORIES (per 1/6 recipe) 60kcal; FAT 0g; CHOL 0mg; SODIUM 0mg; CARB 16g; FIBER 1g; PROTEIN 1g; VIT A 15%; VIT C 140%; CALC 0%; IRON 2%

green beans and potatoes

1 (9-ounce) box frozen cut green beans
1 (20-ounce) package refrigerated red potato wedges
1/2 teaspoon salt
1/8 teaspoon pepper
3 tablespoons garlic butter
2 tablespoons dried parsley

1. Fill large saucepan 1/2 full of water. Cover and bring to a boil on high.
2. Stir beans, potatoes, salt, and pepper into boiling water; cover and return to boil.
3. Reduce heat to medium-high; cook 6–8 minutes, stirring occasionally, or until tender.
4. Drain beans and potatoes; return saucepan to stovetop. Add butter and parsley, stirring until butter melts, using only residual heat. Add beans and potatoes; toss to coat and serve.

CALORIES (per 1/6 recipe) 120kcal; FAT 6g; CHOL 10mg; SODIUM 590mg; CARB 14g; FIBER 3g; PROTEIN 3g; VIT A 8%; VIT C 10%; CALC 2%; IRON 6%

Sweet onions/peppers relish can be found in the Produce department or sometimes with Deli condiments.

shopping list

MEAT

4 boneless pork chops
(3/4-inch thick)

PRODUCE

1 tablespoon roasted potato
seasoning mix

FROZEN

1 (16-ounce) bag succotash

DAIRY

1/3 cup fat-free half-and-half
1 tablespoon butter
1 (20-ounce) bag refrigerated
red potato wedges

DRY GROCERY

1/2 tablespoon
browning sauce
4 drops liquid smoke flavoring
cooking spray
1 1/2 tablespoons country
Dijon mustard
1/3 cup reduced-sodium
chicken broth
1 tablespoon extra-virgin
olive oil
1 teaspoon dried dill weed
1/2 teaspoon seasoned salt

SUGGESTED ITEMS

potato rolls, chocolate cake

pork chops with dijon sauce, roasted dill potatoes, and succotash

MEAL TIME: *40 minutes*

COOKING SEQUENCE

- Prepare potatoes and begin to bake - 10 minutes
- About 10 minutes into bake time, prepare pork chops through step 2 and begin to microwave succotash - 20 minutes
- Complete pork chops and succotash; serve - 10 minutes

SERVES: *4*

SHORTCUTS AND TIPS

Chicken breast cutlets may be substituted for pork. Cooking time will be about the same.

UTENSILS AND COOKWARE

large sauté pan, baking sheet   tongs, cooking spoons
microwave-safe bowl with lid   meat thermometer
mixing bowls, basting brush   measuring utensils

pork chops with dijon sauce

1/2 tablespoon browning sauce

4 drops liquid smoke flavoring

4 boneless pork chops
(3/4-inch thick)

1/2 teaspoon salt

1/8 teaspoon pepper

cooking spray

1 1/2 tablespoons country
Dijon mustard

1/3 cup fat-free half-and-half

1/3 cup reduced-sodium
chicken broth

1. Preheat large sauté pan 2–3 minutes on medium. Combine browning sauce and liquid smoke in small bowl. Brush over both sides of pork chops; season with salt and pepper (wash hands).

2. Coat pan with cooking spray. Add pork chops (wash hands); cook 4 minutes on each side or until nicely browned and internal temperature reaches 160°F (for medium). Use a meat thermometer to accurately ensure doneness.

3. Combine mustard and half-and-half in small bowl.

4. Remove pork chops and set aside. Increase heat to high; add broth to pan, stirring to loosen browned bits of food left on bottom. Stir in mustard mixture and cook 3–4 minutes, stirring occasionally, or until sauce begins to thicken. Serve sauce over pork chops.

CALORIES (per 1/4 recipe) 218kcal; FAT 8g; CHOL 84mg; SODIUM 547mg; CARB 2g; FIBER 0g; PROTEIN 40g; VIT A 1%; VIT C 0%; CALC 2%; IRON 6%

roasted dill potatoes

1 tablespoon roasted potato
seasoning mix (produce)

1 tablespoon extra-virgin olive oil

1 teaspoon dried dill weed

1/4 teaspoon pepper

1 (20-ounce) bag refrigerated red
potato wedges

1. Preheat oven to 400°F. Combine all ingredients (except potatoes) in medium bowl. Add potatoes and toss until coated.

2. Spread in single layer on baking sheet. Bake 25–30 minutes. Serve.

CALORIES (per 1/4 recipe) 118kcal; FAT 3g; CHOL 0mg; SODIUM 730mg; CARB 18g; FIBER 4g; PROTEIN 4g; VIT A 3%; VIT C 6%; CALC 1%; IRON 5%

succotash

1 (16-ounce) bag frozen succotash

1 tablespoon butter

1/2 teaspoon seasoned salt

1. Place succotash in microwave-safe bowl. Cover and microwave on HIGH 8–11 minutes, stirring once, or until tender.

2. Add remaining ingredients. Stir until butter melts and serve.

CALORIES (per 1/4 recipe) 147kcal; FAT 4g; CHOL 8mg; SODIUM 277mg; CARB 26g; FIBER 2g; PROTEIN 5g; VIT A 2%; VIT C 5%; CALC 0%; IRON 2%

shopping list

MEAT

4 boneless pork chops
(3/4-inch thick)

PRODUCE

2 cups plantain chips
1 1/2 cups seedless
red grapes
1 lemon (for juice)
2 teaspoons cilantro
herb paste
2 ounces watercress leaves
(or 1 bunch)

DAIRY

1 egg (or 1/4 cup egg
substitute)
3 tablespoons crumbled
feta cheese

DRY GROCERY

1 (14-ounce) can salad-cut
hearts of palm
6 Cuban (or saltine) crackers
5 tablespoons extra-virgin
olive oil
1/4 cup mayonnaise
1 tablespoon green
pepper sauce
1 teaspoon Complete
seasoning
1 tablespoon flour
1 1/2 tablespoons
peach preserves
large zip-top bag

SUGGESTED ITEMS

white rice, Cuban bread,
custard dessert

plantain-crusted pork chops with sauce and watercress salad

MEAL TIME: *30 minutes*

COOKING SEQUENCE
- Prepare pork chops and begin to cook - 10 minutes
- While pork chops cook, prepare salad - 10 minutes
- Complete pork chops and sauce; serve - 10 minutes

SERVES: *4*

SHORTCUTS AND TIPS

Watercress has a pungent, peppery bite and small, crisp leaves. Use in salads or on sandwiches for a nice change of pace from the usual.

UTENSILS AND COOKWARE

large sauté pan
meat mallet (or rolling pin)
mixing bowls, salad bowl
tongs, cooking spoons

meat thermometer
knife and cutting board
measuring utensils

plantain-crusted pork chops with sauce

2 cups plantain chips

6 Cuban (or saltine) crackers

large zip-top bag

1 egg (or 1/4 cup egg substitute)

4 boneless pork chops
(3/4-inch thick)

1 teaspoon Complete seasoning

1 tablespoon flour

2 tablespoons extra-virgin olive oil

1/4 cup mayonnaise

1 1/2 tablespoons peach preserves

1 tablespoon green pepper sauce

1. Place plantain chips and crackers in large zip-top bag. Crush with meat mallet (or rolling pin). Beat egg lightly in shallow bowl until blended. Sprinkle pork chops with seasoning and flour (wash hands).

2. Preheat large sauté pan on medium 2–3 minutes. Coat pork chops by dipping in egg; remove, let excess drip off, and add to zip-top bag (wash hands). Seal bag tightly and shake (or press with fingertips) to evenly coat pork chops.

3. Place oil in pan; swirl to coat. Add pork chops (wash hands); cook 6–7 minutes on each side or until internal temperature reaches 160°F (for medium). Use a meat thermometer to accurately ensure doneness.

4. While pork chops cook, prepare sauce by combining remaining ingredients in small bowl until blended and smooth. Serve over pork chops or use as a dipping sauce.

CALORIES (per 1/4 recipe) 590kcal; FAT 37g; CHOL 155mg; SODIUM 590mg; CARB 25g; FIBER 2g; PROTEIN 39g; VIT A 2%; VIT C 6%; CALC 2%; IRON 10%

watercress salad

1 lemon (for juice, rinsed)

2 teaspoons cilantro herb paste

3 tablespoons extra-virgin olive oil

2 ounces watercress leaves
(or 1 bunch)

1 (14-ounce) can salad-cut hearts
of palm (drained)

1 1/2 cups seedless red
grapes (rinsed)

3 tablespoons crumbled
feta cheese

1/4 teaspoon salt

1/8 teaspoon pepper

1. Squeeze juice of one-half lemon into salad bowl (about 1 tablespoon). Stir in herb paste and olive oil until blended.

2. Cut (pre-washed and trimmed) watercress into bite-size pieces, if desired, and add to salad bowl. (If using bunch, trim stems and rinse well before cutting to size.)

3. Add remaining ingredients; toss and serve.

CALORIES (per 1/4 recipe) 170kcal; FAT 12g; CHOL 5mg; SODIUM 570mg; CARB 13g; FIBER 2g; PROTEIN 3g; VIT A 25%; VIT C 45%; CALC 10%; IRON 8%

Kids of all ages will have fun crushing the plantain chips and crackers. Be sure the bag is tightly sealed to avoid the possibility of crumbs going everywhere.

shopping list

MEAT

4 boneless pork chops
(3/4-inch thick)

PRODUCE

1 (12-ounce) bag fresh
snipped green beans
1 cup fresh blackberries
(optional)

DAIRY

1 (24-ounce) package
refrigerated mashed
potatoes
1 tablespoon butter
1 tablespoon prepared
horseradish
2 tablespoons sour cream

DRY GROCERY

1 (14-ounce) can
chicken broth
1 teaspoon lemon juice
1 tablespoon cooked
bacon pieces
1 tablespoon soy sauce
olive oil cooking spray
dash cinnamon
dash curry powder
2 teaspoons Montreal steak
seasoning
1/4 cup blackberry preserves

SUGGESTED ITEMS

bread sticks, Boston
cream pie

blackberry pork chops, horseradish mashed potatoes, green beans

MEAL TIME: *30 minutes*

COOKING SEQUENCE

- Preheat grill; prepare beans through step 1 - 5 minutes
- Prepare pork and begin to grill; complete beans - 15 minutes
- Prepare potatoes, complete pork, and serve - 10 minutes

SERVES: *4*

SHORTCUTS AND TIPS

The broth from the green beans makes an excellent base for vegetable soup; freeze up to 1 month.

UTENSILS AND COOKWARE

grill, grilling tongs
small saucepan with lid
medium saucepan with lid
microwave-safe bowl with lid

cooking spoons
meat thermometer
measuring utensils

blackberry pork chops

4 boneless pork chops
(3/4-inch thick)

2 teaspoons Montreal
steak seasoning

olive oil cooking spray

1/4 cup blackberry preserves

1 tablespoon soy sauce

1 teaspoon lemon juice

dash cinnamon

dash curry powder

1 cup fresh blackberries
(optional, rinsed)

1. Preheat grill. Sprinkle both sides of pork with steak seasoning. Coat both sides of pork with cooking spray; place on grill (wash hands). Close lid (or cover loosely with foil); grill 4–5 minutes on each side or until internal temperature reaches 160°F (for medium). Use a meat thermometer to accurately ensure doneness.

2. Combine remaining ingredients (except blackberries) in small saucepan. Bring just to boiling on medium, stirring occasionally, to liquefy preserves. Cover and remove from heat.

3. Ladle sauce over pork chops and garnish with blackberries. Serve.

CALORIES (per 1/4 recipe) 300kcal; FAT 10g; CHOL 95mg; SODIUM 870mg; CARB 13g; FIBER 0g; PROTEIN 37g; VIT A 0%; VIT C 0%; CALC 2%; IRON 6%

horseradish mashed potatoes

1 (24-ounce) package refrigerated
mashed potatoes

2 tablespoons sour cream

1 tablespoon butter

1 tablespoon prepared horseradish

1. Place potatoes in microwave-safe bowl; cover and microwave on HIGH 3 minutes.

2. Stir in remaining ingredients. Microwave on HIGH 3 more minutes or until thoroughly heated. Stir and serve.

CALORIES (per 1/4 recipe) 250kcal; FAT 16g; CHOL 35mg; SODIUM 660mg; CARB 21g; FIBER 1g; PROTEIN 3g; VIT A 15%; VIT C 2%; CALC 6%; IRON 2%

green beans

1 (12-ounce) bag fresh snipped
green beans (rinsed)

1 (14-ounce) can chicken broth

1 tablespoon cooked bacon pieces

1/4 teaspoon salt

1/8 teaspoon pepper

1. Combine all ingredients in medium saucepan on high; cover and bring to boil.

2. Reduce heat to medium; cook 10–15 minutes, stirring occasionally, or until beans are desired tenderness. Serve.

CALORIES (per 1/4 recipe) 40kcal; FAT 1g; CHOL 5mg; SODIUM 660mg; CARB 7g; FIBER 3g; PROTEIN 3g; VIT A 10%; VIT C 25%; CALC 4%; IRON 6%

Spices usually associated with desserts, such as cinnamon and cloves, are delicious additions to pork dishes.

shopping list

MEAT

1 pork shoulder roast
(about 4 lb)
2 cured chorizo links
(about 3 oz)

PRODUCE

2 large bell peppers
8 fresh garlic cloves
1 lemon (for juice)

DAIRY

1 (20-ounce) package
homestyle sliced potatoes

DRY GROCERY

aluminum foil
1 1/2 teaspoons adobo
seasoning (Spanish
seasoned salt)
olive oil cooking spray
1 (4.5-ounce) can chopped
green chiles

SUGGESTED ITEMS

Cuban bread, flan
(custard dessert)

slow cooker pork roast, fried potatoes, and broiled peppers

MEAL TIME: *8 to 10 hours*

COOKING SEQUENCE

- Prepare pork and begin to slow cook - 10 minutes
- Allow pork to slow cook - 8 to 10 hours
- 25 minutes before serving, prepare potatoes and peppers; serve - 25 minutes

SERVES: *4 (with leftovers)*

SHORTCUTS AND TIPS

It's okay to choose a pork roast with a layer of visible fat. The slow-cooking process breaks down the fat, self-basting the meat, and yields a tender, moist roast.

UTENSILS AND COOKWARE

slow cooker, baking sheet   knife and cutting board
large sauté pan with lid   measuring utensils
garlic press, cooking spoon

slow cooker pork roast

olive oil cooking spray

1 pork shoulder roast (about 4 lb)

1 teaspoon adobo seasoning
(Spanish seasoned salt)

1/4 teaspoon pepper

6 fresh garlic cloves

2 cured chorizo links (about 3 oz)

1 (4.5-ounce) can chopped green
chiles (undrained)

1. Coat slow cooker with cooking spray; preheat on high. Cut 10–12 one-half-inch-deep slits into fat side of pork, about 1–2 inches apart. Sprinkle roast with adobo seasoning and pepper; place in slow cooker (fat side up).
2. Crush garlic, using garlic press, over top of pork. Use knife to remove garlic from bottom of press. Rub garlic into pork, pressing into slits (wash hands).
3. Slice chorizo lengthwise, then into 1/4-inch-thick pieces; sprinkle over pork (wash hands). Spread chiles over top of pork. Reduce heat to low; cover and cook 8–10 hours or until tender. Serve. (Makes 6 servings.)

CALORIES (per 1/6 recipe) 310kcal; FAT 16g; CHOL 125mg; SODIUM 630mg; CARB 2g; FIBER 1g; PROTEIN 37g; VIT A 0%; VIT C 10%; CALC 4%; IRON 15%

fried potatoes

olive oil cooking spray

1 (20-ounce) package homestyle
sliced potatoes

1/4 teaspoon salt

1/8 teaspoon pepper

1 lemon (for juice, rinsed)

1. Preheat large sauté pan on medium-high 2–3 minutes.
2. Remove pan from heat and coat with cooking spray. Add potatoes; coat top of potatoes with cooking spray and season with salt and pepper. Cover and cook 8–12 minutes, turning often, or until tender and golden.
3. Squeeze juice of one-half lemon over potatoes; toss to coat and serve.

CALORIES (per 1/4 recipe) 100kcal; FAT 0g; CHOL 0mg; SODIUM 330mg; CARB 23g; FIBER 1g; PROTEIN 3g; VIT A 0%; VIT C 4%; CALC 0%; IRON 2%

broiled peppers

aluminum foil

2 large bell peppers (rinsed)

2 fresh garlic cloves

1/2 teaspoon adobo seasoning
(Spanish seasoned salt)

1/8 teaspoon pepper

olive oil cooking spray

1. Place oven rack 6 inches from broiler, then preheat oven on broil. Line baking sheet with foil. Cut peppers in half; remove seeds. Place on baking sheet (cut side up).
2. Crush garlic, using garlic press, into peppers. Use knife to remove garlic from bottom of press. Spread garlic evenly over peppers. Sprinkle each pepper with adobo seasoning and pepper.
3. Coat top of peppers with cooking spray. Broil 6–8 minutes or until edges are dark brown. Remove from oven, cover tightly with foil, and let stand 6 minutes. Slice and serve.

CALORIES (per 1/4 recipe) 20kcal; FAT 0g; CHOL 0mg; SODIUM 180mg; CARB 4g; FIBER 1g; PROTEIN 1g; VIT A 6%; VIT C 110%; CALC 2%; IRON 2%

Chorizo can be found both fresh (raw) and cured (or dry). This recipe uses the dry, cured style.

shopping list

MEAT
1 lb beef, cut for stew

BAKERY
8 corn muffins

FROZEN
2 cups seasoning blend (diced onions, bell peppers, celery)

DAIRY
1/4 cup butter
2 tablespoons whole milk

DRY GROCERY
1 (10-ounce) can milder diced tomatoes and green chiles
1 (14.5-ounce) can diced tomatoes with garlic/onion
2 (16-ounce) cans pinto beans
1 cup refried beans
1 tablespoon chopped green chiles
1 packet taco seasoning mix (about 1 ounce)
1 teaspoon green pepper sauce
2 tablespoons honey
large zip-top bag

SUGGESTED ITEMS
shredded cheese (to top stew), fresh salad blend, lemon meringue pie

cowboy stew and corn muffins with sweet chile butter

MEAL TIME: *8 to 10 hours*

COOKING SEQUENCE
- Prepare stew and begin to slow cook - 5 minutes
- Allow stew to slow cook - 8 to 10 hours
- 10 minutes before serving, prepare corn muffins and serve - 10 minutes

SERVES: *8*

SHORTCUTS AND TIPS
Use this recipe to make hearty nachos topped with cheese and sour cream.

UTENSILS AND COOKWARE
slow cooker   cooking spoons
microwave-safe dish   measuring utensils
small microwave-safe bowl

cowboy stew

1 lb beef, cut for stew

1 packet taco seasoning mix (about 1 ounce)

large zip-top bag

1 (14.5-ounce) can diced tomatoes with garlic/onion (undrained)

1 (10-ounce) can milder diced tomatoes and green chiles (undrained)

1 cup refried beans

2 cups frozen seasoning blend (diced onions, bell peppers, celery)

2 (16-ounce) cans pinto beans (drained)

1. Preheat slow cooker on high. Place beef and taco seasoning in zip-top bag; shake to coat. Transfer beef and seasoning to slow cooker.
2. Stir in canned tomatoes (including liquid), refried beans, and seasoning blend.
3. Pour beans on top of beef mixture (do not stir). Cover and reduce heat to low; cook 8 to 10 hours. Serve.

CALORIES (per 1/8 recipe) 280kcal; FAT 7g; CHOL 35mg; SODIUM 1230mg; CARB 29g; FIBER 8g; PROTEIN 19g; VIT A 10%; VIT C 10%; CALC 6%; IRON 20%

corn muffins with sweet chile butter

1/4 cup butter

2 tablespoons whole milk

1 tablespoon chopped green chiles

2 tablespoons honey

1 teaspoon green pepper sauce

8 Bakery corn muffins

1. Place all ingredients (except muffins) in small microwave-safe bowl. Microwave on HIGH for 20 seconds; stir and microwave 10–20 more seconds or until butter melts.
2. Place muffins (in paper liners) in microwave-safe dish. Cut a deep "X" in muffins, pull apart slightly, and drizzle sauce over cut muffins.
3. Microwave 20–30 seconds or until warmed. Serve.

CALORIES (per 1/8 recipe) 280kcal; FAT 12g; CHOL 35mg; SODIUM 420mg; CARB 41g; FIBER 2g; PROTEIN 4g; VIT A 8%; VIT C 2%; CALC 6%; IRON 10%

Slow cookers are great for busy families. Spend just a few minutes in the morning and come home later that evening to find that dinner is almost ready.

poultry perfection

chicken ponzu over rice
(recipe on page 66)

cajun-spiced tenders
(recipe on page 68)

a flock of fabulous flavors

Chicken and turkey are marvelously versatile, and in this section are well over a dozen different ways we love to prepare them. You'll find delicious tastes hailing from Asia, America, Italy, and the Islands of the Caribbean Sea, each one earning the enthusiastic accolades of our staff. We believe you and your family will be similarly impressed.

shopping list

MEAT

4 (5-ounce) tomato/basil
  boneless, skinless
  chicken breasts

BAKERY

4 coconut pecan
  bite-size cookies

PRODUCE

4 peaches
2–3 ounces baby arugula
  leaves (2 cups)

DAIRY

1/2 cup aerosol
  whipped cream
2 tablespoons butter
2 tablespoons shredded
  Parmesan cheese

DRY GROCERY

1 tablespoon sugar
cooking spray
1/4 cup caramel topping
8 ounces multigrain
  thin spaghetti
1/3 cup sun-dried
  tomato pesto
1 tablespoon capers

SUGGESTED ITEMS

cucumber and tomato salad,
  Italian bread

chicken angelina with peach meltdown

MEAL TIME: *35 minutes*

COOKING SEQUENCE

- Prepare peaches through step 1 - 10 minutes
- Begin to grill peaches; prepare chicken and begin to grill (turn peaches) - 5 minutes
- Complete chicken and serve - 20 minutes
- Assemble dessert when ready to serve

SERVES: *4*

SHORTCUTS AND TIPS

Cut the grilled peaches into bite-size pieces. Layer with remaining ingredients in large wine glasses, for an elegant presentation.

UTENSILS AND COOKWARE

grill, grilling tongs
large saucepan with lid
4 dessert dishes
cooking spoon

meat thermometer
knife and cutting board
measuring utensils

chicken angelina

8 ounces multigrain thin spaghetti

2 1/2 cups water

1/3 cup sun-dried tomato pesto

1 tablespoon capers

2 tablespoons butter

4 (5-ounce) tomato/basil boneless, skinless chicken breasts

2–3 ounces baby arugula leaves (2 cups)

2 tablespoons shredded Parmesan cheese

1. Preheat grill. Meanwhile, break pasta in half while placing in large saucepan. Stir in water, tomato pesto, capers, and butter. Cover and bring to boil on medium-high, stirring often.

2. Place chicken on grill (wash hands); close lid (or cover loosely with foil). Grill 6–7 minutes, turning occasionally, or until internal temperature reaches 165°F. Use a meat thermometer to accurately ensure doneness.

3. When pasta boils, reduce to medium and cook 6–9 minutes, stirring often, or until most of liquid is absorbed.

4. Stir arugula into pasta and cook 1–2 more minutes, stirring often, or until leaves are wilted. Slice chicken thinly and arrange over pasta. Sprinkle with cheese and serve.

CALORIES (per 1/4 recipe) 440kcal; FAT 11g; CHOL 83mg; SODIUM 1041mg; CARB 45g; FIBER 5g; PROTEIN 39g; VIT A 32%; VIT C 12%; CALC 11%; IRON 18%

peach meltdown

4 peaches (rinsed)

1 tablespoon sugar

cooking spray

4 Bakery coconut pecan bite-size cookies

1/2 cup aerosol whipped cream

1/4 cup caramel topping

1. Preheat grill. Cut peaches in half; remove and discard pits. Sprinkle cut sides of peaches with sugar; let stand 5 minutes.

2. Coat cut side of peaches with cooking spray. Place on grill with cut side down; close lid (or cover loosely with foil) and grill 3–5 minutes or until browned.

3. Turn peaches; cover and cook 3–7 more minutes or until desired tenderness. (Grill times may vary widely depending on ripeness of peaches.) Skin of peaches can be easily removed but is not necessary. To remove skin, gently squeeze each cooked peach half with fingertips until skin separates from peach; discard skin.

4. Crumble cookies into four dessert dishes and top each with 1 tablespoon of the whipped topping. Add peach halves; drizzle each dessert with 1 tablespoon caramel sauce and top with 1 tablespoon whipped topping. Serve.

CALORIES (per 1/4 recipe) 254kcal; FAT 10g; CHOL 20mg; SODIUM 135mg; CARB 38g; FIBER 3g; PROTEIN 2g; VIT A 13%; VIT C 10%; CALC 1%; IRON 3%

Arugula is an aromatic salad green with a peppery, mustard flavor (also known as Italian cress or rocket). It's rich in iron and vitamins A and C. Baby spinach leaves can be used for a milder flavor.

shopping list

MEAT

4 (5-ounce) Italian herb
  boneless, skinless
  chicken breasts

PRODUCE

1/2 cup pre-diced
  fresh tomatoes
1/2 cup baby arugula leaves
1 tablespoon + 2 teaspoons
  roasted garlic
1 lb rapini
1/4 cup pre-diced red onions

DAIRY

4 ounces fresh
  mozzarella cheese
3 tablespoons shredded
  Parmesan cheese

DRY GROCERY

1 (8-ounce) package
  seasoned risotto mix
4 tablespoons extra-virgin
  olive oil
1/4 cup light olive oil
  vinaigrette
1/4 cup roasted red peppers
1/2 cup plain bread crumbs

SUGGESTED ITEMS

baguette, chocolate cake

bruschetta chicken over risotto with rapini italiano

MEAL TIME: *40 minutes*

COOKING SEQUENCE
- Prepare chicken recipe through step 1; begin to boil water for rapini - 5 minutes
- Prepare topping for chicken (step 2); continue rapini through step 2 - 10 minutes
- Complete chicken and rapini; serve - 25 minutes

SERVES: *4*

SHORTCUT AND TIPS
Serve the bruschetta topping on crusty French bread for a delicious addition to any meal.

UTENSILS AND COOKWARE

large saucepan with lid   cooking spoons
medium saucepan with lid   meat thermometer
large sauté pan with lid   knife and cutting board
medium bowls, colander, tongs   measuring utensils

bruschetta chicken over risotto

2 1/2 cups water

1 (8-ounce) package seasoned risotto mix

2 tablespoons extra-virgin olive oil, divided

1/2 cup pre-diced fresh tomatoes

1/4 cup light olive oil vinaigrette

1/4 cup roasted red peppers

1/2 cup baby arugula leaves

4 ounces fresh mozzarella cheese

1/2 teaspoon salt

1/8 teaspoon pepper

1/2 cup bread crumbs

2 tablespoons shredded Parmesan cheese, divided

4 (5-ounce) Italian herb boneless, skinless chicken breasts

2 teaspoons roasted garlic

1. Combine water, risotto mix, and 1 tablespoon of the olive oil in medium saucepan; cover and bring to a boil on high. Boil 3 minutes, stirring occasionally. Reduce heat to low; cover and cook 15 minutes, stirring occasionally.

2. Combine tomatoes and vinaigrette in medium bowl. Cut peppers, arugula, and mozzarella cheese into 1/4-inch pieces; add to tomato mixture. Season with salt and pepper; toss to blend. Set aside.

3. Preheat large sauté pan on medium 2–3 minutes. Combine bread crumbs and 1 tablespoon of the Parmesan cheese in medium bowl. Dredge chicken in bread crumb mixture, pressing down with fingers to coat; wash hands. Place remaining 1 tablespoon oil in pan; swirl to coat. Add chicken (wash hands); cover and cook 5–7 minutes on each side or until golden and internal temperature reaches 165°F. Use a meat thermometer to accurately ensure doneness.

4. Stir roasted garlic and remaining 1 tablespoon Parmesan cheese into risotto. Cover and cook 2–3 more minutes, stirring occasionally, or until rice is creamy and tender. Top chicken with tomato mixture and serve over risotto.

CALORIES (per 1/4 recipe) 593kcal; FAT 20g; CHOL 93mg; SODIUM 2119mg; CARB 57g; FIBER 2g; PROTEIN 42g; VIT A 22%; VIT C 31%; CALC 20%; IRON 17%

rapini italiano

1 lb rapini (rinsed)

2 tablespoons extra-virgin olive oil

1/4 cup pre-diced red onions

1 tablespoon roasted garlic

1 tablespoon shredded Parmesan cheese

1. Fill large saucepan half full of water. Cover and bring to a boil on high for rapini. Cut 3–4 inches of the stem off rapini, leaving leafy tops only; discard stems.

2. Stir rapini into boiling water. Boil 3–4 minutes, stirring occasionally, or until tender. Rinse with cold water; drain thoroughly.

3. Return same large saucepan to stove. Heat on medium-high 2–3 minutes. Place oil in pan; swirl to coat. Add onions and garlic; cook 2–3 minutes to brown.

4. Stir in rapini, turning to coat with oil; cook 6–8 more minutes, stirring occasionally, or until flavors are well blended. Sprinkle with cheese and serve.

CALORIES (per 1/4 recipe) 99kcal; FAT 8g; CHOL 2mg; SODIUM 75mg; CARB 4g; FIBER 3g; PROTEIN 4g; VIT A 60%; VIT C 39%; CALC 15%; IRON 14%

Rapini is a leafy green vegetable used in Italian and Chinese cuisine. It is also known as broccoli rabe (raab) although it is not related to broccoli. It is related to cabbage and turnips. It is pungent, a bit nutty, and has a slight, but pleasantly bitter flavor.

shopping list

MEAT

4 boneless chicken cutlets
    (about 1 lb)

PRODUCE

1 lemon (for juice)
1 lb fresh asparagus spears

DAIRY

6 tablespoons butter

DRY GROCERY

1 (5.6-ounce) box toasted
    pine nut (or seasoned)
    couscous
1 tablespoon flour
1 1/2 teaspoons seasoned salt
large zip-top bag
1 tablespoon capers

SUGGESTED ITEMS

fresh salad blend, dinner rolls,
    fruit pie

chicken piccata with couscous and quick asparagus

MEAL TIME: *25 minutes*

COOKING SEQUENCE

- Prepare asparagus through step 1 - 10 minutes
- Prepare chicken and couscous through step 3 - 10 minutes
- Complete asparagus and chicken; serve - 5 minutes

SERVES: *4*

SHORTCUT AND TIPS

The Chicken Piccata may also be served over angel hair pasta for a more traditional presentation.

UTENSILS

large sauté pan
medium saucepan with lid
microwave-safe bowl with lid
tongs, cooking spoons

meat thermometer
knife and cutting board
measuring utensils

chicken piccata with couscous

1 3/4 cups water, divided

1 (5.6-ounce) box toasted pine nut (or seasoned) couscous

5 tablespoons butter, divided

1 tablespoon flour

1 teaspoon seasoned salt

large zip-top bag

4 boneless chicken cutlets (about 1 lb)

1 tablespoon capers

1/2 lemon (for juice, rinsed)

1. Place in medium saucepan, 1 1/2 cups of the water, contents of spice packet (from couscous), and 2 tablespoons of the butter; bring to a boil on high for couscous.

2. Place flour and seasoned salt in zip-top bag; shake to mix. Add chicken (wash hands); seal tightly and shake to coat. Preheat large sauté pan on medium-high 2–3 minutes. Add 2 tablespoons of the butter; swirl to coat. Add chicken (wash hands); cook 5 minutes, without turning, or until golden.

3. Meanwhile, stir couscous into boiling water; cover, remove from heat, and set aside.

4. Turn chicken. Stir in capers, juice of one-half lemon (about 1 tablespoon), remaining 1 tablespoon butter, and remaining 1/4 cup water. Cook 2–3 minutes or until sauce begins to thicken and internal temperature of chicken reaches 165°F. Use a meat thermometer to accurately ensure doneness. Fluff couscous with fork and serve.

CALORIES (per 1/4 recipe) 400kcal; FAT 17g; CHOL 105mg; SODIUM 940mg; CARB 30g; FIBER 2g; PROTEIN 32g; VIT A 10%; VIT C 8%; CALC 2%; IRON 8%

quick asparagus

1 lb fresh asparagus spears (rinsed)

1 tablespoon water

1 tablespoon butter

1/2 teaspoon seasoned salt

1. Cut 1 inch from tough root end of asparagus spears and discard. To do this quickly, group half the spears together, align ends, and slice with sharp knife. Cut into 2-inch pieces. Place in microwave-safe bowl with water.

2. Cover and microwave on HIGH 4–5 minutes, stirring once, or until desired tenderness. Drain asparagus; stir in butter and seasoned salt. Serve.

CALORIES (per 1/4 recipe) 50kcal; FAT 3g; CHOL 10mg; SODIUM 210mg; CARB 4g; FIBER 2g; PROTEIN 2g; VIT A 20%; VIT C 10%; CALC 2%; IRON 15%

Capers are a type of handpicked, unopened flower buds that have been pickled in a vinegar brine. They have a tangy flavor and are used in sauces and as a garnish in meat recipes. Some people choose to rinse capers to remove some of the saltiness; however, rinsing won't change the actual flavor of the capers.

shopping list

MEAT

4 boneless, skinless chicken
   breasts or cutlets (1 3/4 lb)

PRODUCE

1/2 cup + 2 tablespoons
   pre-diced onions
4 ounces pre-sliced baby
   portabella mushrooms
3 fresh garlic cloves
2 (10-ounce) containers
   pre-sliced zucchini (5 cups)

FROZEN

1 (16-ounce) package
   cavatelli pasta

DELI

2 tablespoons shredded
   Asiago cheese

DRY GROCERY

1/2 teaspoon dried
   thyme leaves
3 tablespoons extra-virgin
   olive oil
1/4 cup Marsala wine
1/2 cup reduced-sodium
   chicken broth
1 packet mushroom gravy mix
   (about .75-ounce)

SUGGESTED ITEMS

Italian bread, cannoli

chicken marsala, pasta olio, and zucchini milanese

MEAL TIME: *25 minutes*

COOKING SEQUENCE

- Prepare pasta and begin to bring to a boil - 10 minutes
- Prepare chicken and begin to brown - 5 minutes
- Complete pasta, prepare zucchini, complete chicken and serve - 10 minutes

SERVES: *4*

SHORTCUT AND TIPS

Browning the mushrooms and onions will intensify the rich mushroom flavor.

UTENSILS AND COOKWARE

large saucepan with lid   cooking spoons
large sauté pan   meat thermometer
microwave-safe bowl   measuring utensils
tongs, garlic press

chicken marsala

4 boneless, skinless chicken breasts or cutlets (1 3/4 lb)

1/2 teaspoon dried thyme leaves

1 tablespoon extra-virgin olive oil

1/2 cup pre-diced onions

4 ounces pre-sliced baby portabella mushrooms (rinsed)

1/4 cup Marsala wine

1/2 cup reduced-sodium chicken broth

1 packet mushroom gravy mix (about .75-ounce)

1. Preheat large sauté pan on medium-high 2–3 minutes. Sprinkle both sides of chicken with thyme (wash hands).

2. Place oil in pan; swirl to coat. Add onions and mushrooms; cook 3–4 minutes or until tender. Move onions and mushrooms to outer edge of pan. Place chicken in center of pan (wash hands); cook 2–3 minutes on each side until browned.

3. Stir in wine, then stir in remaining ingredients until well blended. Reduce heat to low; cook 6–8 minutes or until sauce thickens and internal temperature of chicken reaches 165°F. Use a meat thermometer to accurately ensure doneness. Serve.

CALORIES (per 1/4 recipe) 310kcal; FAT 6g; CHOL 115mg; SODIUM 500mg; CARB 9g; FIBER 1g; PROTEIN 48g; VIT A 0%; VIT C 6%; CALC 4%; IRON 10%

pasta olio

1 1/4 cups water

1 (16-ounce) package frozen cavatelli pasta

1 tablespoon extra-virgin olive oil

1/2 teaspoon salt

3 fresh garlic cloves

1 tablespoon shredded Asiago cheese

1. Place water, pasta, oil, and salt in large saucepan. Cover and bring to boil on high. Reduce heat to medium; cook 3–4 more minutes or until most of liquid is absorbed and pasta is tender.

2. Crush garlic, using garlic press, into pasta. Use knife to remove garlic from bottom of press. Stir, cover, and remove from heat; let stand 5 minutes or until remaining liquid is absorbed.

3. Stir, sprinkle with cheese, and serve.

CALORIES (per 1/4 recipe) 343kcal; FAT 5g; CHOL 13mg; SODIUM 305mg; CARB 61g; FIBER 7g; PROTEIN 13g; VIT A 1%; VIT C 6%; CALC 5%; IRON 12%

zucchini milanese

2 (10-ounce) containers pre-sliced zucchini (5 cups)

2 tablespoons pre-diced onions

1 tablespoon extra-virgin olive oil

1/2 teaspoon salt

1 tablespoon shredded Asiago cheese

1. Place all ingredients (except cheese) in microwave-safe bowl.

2. Microwave on HIGH 6 minutes, stirring once, or until tender. Stir, sprinkle with cheese, and serve.

CALORIES (per 1/4 recipe) 59kcal; FAT 4g; CHOL 2mg; SODIUM 295mg; CARB 5g; FIBER 2g; PROTEIN 2g; VIT A 10%; VIT C 22%; CALC 4%; IRON 4%

shopping list

MEAT
1 lb boneless chicken cutlets

PRODUCE
1 bag fresh baby spinach
  leaves (5–6 oz)
1/2 cup grape tomatoes
  or pre-diced tomatoes

DRY GROCERY
1 (11-ounce) can mandarin
  oranges (about 1 cup)
1 (10-ounce) can milder diced
  tomatoes and green chiles
8 ounces orzo pasta
1 packet onion gravy mix
  (about 1 oz)
1/4 cup raspberry vinaigrette
1/4 cup mayonnaise

SUGGESTED ITEMS
Bakery bread or dinner rolls,
  Key lime pie

zesty chicken orzo with spinach raspberry salad

MEAL TIME: *15 minutes*

15 MINUTE Meal Idea
Serve four in 15 minutes!

COOKING SEQUENCE
- Prepare chicken through step 2 - 5 minutes
- While chicken cooks, prepare salad - 5 minutes
- Complete chicken and serve - 5 minutes

SERVES: 4

SHORTCUT AND TIPS
No orzo pasta on hand? Simply replace with an equal amount of instant rice and reduce final cook time to 1–2 minutes.

UTENSILS AND COOKWARE
large sauté pan with lid
salad bowl
medium bowl

tongs, cooking spoon
knife and cutting board
measuring utensils

zesty chicken orzo

1/4 cup mayonnaise

1 packet onion gravy mix (about 1 oz)

1 lb boneless chicken cutlets

1 1/2 cups water

1 (10-ounce) can milder diced tomatoes and green chiles (undrained)

8 ounces orzo pasta

1. Preheat large sauté pan on medium-high 1–2 minutes. Combine mayonnaise and dry gravy mix in medium bowl. Stir in chicken until evenly coated. Add chicken mixture to pan; cook chicken 1 minute on each side or until lightly browned.

2. Stir in water, tomatoes (undrained), and orzo until all ingredients are well blended. Cover and cook 4 minutes, stirring occasionally, or until hot and bubbly.

3. Reduce to medium; cook (covered) 4–5 minutes, stirring occasionally, or until most of liquid is absorbed and orzo is tender. Serve.

CALORIES (per 1/4 recipe) 460kcal; FAT 14g; CHOL 70mg; SODIUM 760mg; CARB 49g; FIBER 2g; PROTEIN 35g; VIT A 6%; VIT C 8%; CALC 4%; IRON 15%

spinach raspberry salad

1 bag fresh baby spinach leaves (5–6 oz)

1 (11-ounce) can mandarin oranges (about 1 cup; well drained)

1/2 cup grape tomatoes (rinsed) or pre-diced tomatoes

1/4 cup raspberry vinaigrette

1. Place all ingredients (except dressing) in salad bowl.

2. Add dressing; toss and serve.

CALORIES (per 1/4 recipe) 100kcal; FAT 2.5g; CHOL 0mg; SODIUM 210mg; CARB 20g; FIBER 3g; PROTEIN 1g; VIT A 45%; VIT C 35%; CALC 4%; IRON 10%

Chicken cutlets are thin, tender slices of boneless chicken breast. They cook quickly and make a great last-minute meal solution.

shopping list

MEAT

4 boneless, skinless chicken
  breasts or cutlets (1 3/4 lb)

PRODUCE

1/4 cup pre-diced
  fresh tomatoes
1/4 cup pre-diced green
  bell peppers
1/4 cup pre-diced red onions

DAIRY

2 cups shredded
  Cheddar cheese

DRY GROCERY

3 tablespoons canola oil
1/2 cup chicken breading mix
2 teaspoons vegetable
  seasoning blend
1 packet country gravy mix
  (.7 ounce)
2 cups instant grits

SUGGESTED ITEMS

okra, cornbread, apple pie

country garden chicken with cheesy grits

MEAL TIME: *25 minutes*

COOKING SEQUENCE

- Bread chicken and begin to cook - 10 minutes
- While chicken cooks, prepare grits; complete chicken and serve - 15 minutes

SERVES: *4*

SHORTCUT AND TIPS

You can cut the carbs by about 50% in the chicken recipe by pan-frying the chicken without the breading.

UTENSILS AND COOKWARE

large sauté pan   tongs
microwave-safe bowl with lid   cooking spoons
mixing bowl   measuring utensils

country garden chicken

3 tablespoons canola oil

4 boneless, skinless chicken breasts or cutlets (1 3/4 lb)

1 2/3 cups water, divided

1/2 cup chicken breading mix

1/4 cup pre-diced fresh tomatoes

1/4 cup pre-diced green bell peppers

1/4 cup pre-diced red onions

2 teaspoons vegetable seasoning blend

1 packet country gravy mix (.7 ounce)

1. Place oil in large sauté pan and heat on medium-high 2–3 minutes.
2. Moisten chicken with 1 tablespoon of the water. Place breading mix in bowl. Coat chicken, one piece at a time, by pressing into breading mix; turn and coat other side. (For thicker breading, coat twice.) Set chicken aside (wash hands).
3. Place chicken carefully in hot oil (wash hands); cook 6–8 minutes, turning occasionally, or until crisp and golden brown. Remove chicken from pan; cover to keep warm.
4. Stir tomatoes, green peppers, onions, and vegetable seasoning into pan with drippings. Heat on medium-high 2–3 minutes or until onions are translucent. Stir in gravy mix and gradually add remaining 1 1/2 cups water, stirring continuously, or until sauce is smooth. Reduce heat to low; cook 2–3 minutes, stirring often, or until thoroughly heated. Serve sauce over chicken.

CALORIES (per 1/4 recipe) 400kcal; FAT 15g; CHOL 115mg; SODIUM 900mg; CARB 14g; FIBER 0g; PROTEIN 47g; VIT A 4%; VIT C 20%; CALC 2%; IRON 8%

cheesy grits

2 1/2 cups water

2 cups instant grits

2 cups shredded Cheddar cheese

1. Combine all ingredients in microwave-safe bowl.
2. Cover and microwave on HIGH 6 minutes, stirring once, or until water is absorbed. Stir and serve. (Makes 6 servings.)

CALORIES (per 1/6 recipe) 340kcal; FAT 13g; CHOL 40mg; SODIUM 244mg; CARB 43g; FIBER 0g; PROTEIN 14g; VIT A 13%; VIT C 0%; CALC 26%; IRON 11%

Always be sure to use clean serving plates and clean serving utensils. The ones that held or even turned the meat while cooking should not be reused in order to help avoid any cross-contamination from the raw meat.

shopping list

MEAT
4 chicken fillets (1 3/4 lb)

PRODUCE
1 bag fresh spinach leaves
  (8–10 oz)

DAIRY
1 tablespoon butter

DRY GROCERY
2 tablespoons flour
1 teaspoon seasoned salt
large zip-top bag
butter cooking spray
1 (11-ounce) can mandarin
  oranges (about 1 cup)
2 tablespoons
  orange marmalade
2 teaspoons cornstarch
1 teaspoon lite soy sauce
1 (14-ounce) can chicken
  broth with roasted garlic
1 cup basmati rice
3 tablespoons
  diced pimientos

SUGGESTED ITEMS
sourdough rolls, carrot cake

orange-glazed chicken, seasoned basmati rice, and fresh spinach

MEAL TIME: *25 minutes*

COOKING SEQUENCE
- Prepare rice through step 1; prepare chicken through step 2 - 5 minutes
- Continue rice through step 2; continue chicken through step 4 - 10 minutes
- Prepare spinach and complete rice; serve - 10 minutes

SERVES: 4

SHORTCUT AND TIPS
Try this recipe with boneless pork chops or fish.

UTENSILS AND COOKWARE
large sauté pan with lid
medium saucepan with lid
microwave-safe bowl with lid

mixing bowl
cooking spoons, tongs
measuring utensils

orange-glazed chicken

2 tablespoons flour

1 teaspoon seasoned salt

large zip-top bag

4 chicken fillets (1 3/4 lb)

butter cooking spray

1 (11-ounce) can mandarin oranges (about 1 cup; undrained)

2 tablespoons orange marmalade

2 teaspoons cornstarch

1 teaspoon lite soy sauce

1. Preheat large sauté pan on medium-high 2–3 minutes. Place flour and seasoned salt in zip-top bag and shake to mix. Add chicken (wash hands); seal tightly and shake to coat. Knead bag to coat chicken.
2. Coat pan with cooking spray. Add chicken (wash hands); coat top of chicken with cooking spray. Cover and cook 4 minutes on each side.
3. Meanwhile, in medium bowl, gently stir remaining ingredients together.
4. Turn chicken again and add orange mixture. Reduce heat to medium; cook 5 minutes, turning chicken once, or until mixture is thoroughly heated. Serve.

CALORIES (per 1/4 recipe) 310kcal; FAT 3g; CHOL 115mg; SODIUM 540mg; CARB 24g; FIBER 1g; PROTEIN 47g; VIT A 15%; VIT C 30%; CALC 4%; IRON 10%

seasoned basmati rice

1 (14-ounce) can chicken broth with roasted garlic

3 tablespoons diced pimientos (undrained)

1 cup basmati rice

1. Combine all ingredients in medium saucepan; cover and bring to boil on high.
2. Stir once and reduce heat to medium-low; cover and cook 15 minutes.
3. Remove from heat and let stand 5 minutes. Serve.

CALORIES (per 1/4 recipe) 165kcal; FAT 1g; CHOL 0mg; SODIUM 425mg; CARB 35g; FIBER 0g; PROTEIN 4g; VIT A 7%; VIT C 15%; CALC 0%; IRON 10%

fresh spinach

1 bag fresh spinach leaves (8–10 oz)

1 tablespoon butter

1/4 teaspoon salt

1/8 teaspoon pepper

1. Place spinach in microwave-safe bowl. Cover and microwave on HIGH 2–3 minutes.
2. Drain spinach; stir in remaining ingredients and serve.

CALORIES (per 1/4 recipe) 40kcal; FAT 3g; CHOL 10mg; SODIUM 80mg; CARB 3g; FIBER 2g; PROTEIN 2g; VIT A 130%; VIT C 35%; CALC 8%; IRON 10%

shopping list

MEAT
1 1/2 lb boneless, skinless chicken breasts

PRODUCE
4–6 fresh chives

FROZEN
3 cups broccoli florets

DAIRY
2 tablespoons butter
1 (10-ounce) container refrigerated light Alfredo sauce
2 tablespoons shredded Parmesan cheese, optional

DRY GROCERY
2 tablespoons flour
1/2 teaspoon seasoned salt
large zip-top bag
1/4 cup white wine
2 (8.8-ounce) pouches pre-cooked chicken-flavored rice

SUGGESTED ITEMS
sliced tomatoes, fresh salad blend, biscuits, fruit pie

chicken divan with aromatic rice

MEAL TIME: *25 minutes*

COOKING SEQUENCE
• Prepare chicken and begin to cook - 10 minutes
• Prepare rice and complete chicken; serve - 15 minutes

SERVES: *4*

SHORTCUT AND TIPS
Chives can be quickly snipped by using kitchen shears.

UTENSILS AND COOKWARE
large sauté pan with lid	tongs, cooking spoons
microwave-safe bowl with lid	knife and cutting board
kitchen shears	measuring utensils

chicken divan

2 tablespoons flour

1/2 teaspoon seasoned salt

large zip-top bag

1 1/2 lb boneless, skinless chicken breasts

1 tablespoon butter

3 cups frozen broccoli florets

1 (10-ounce) container refrigerated light Alfredo sauce

1/4 cup white wine

2 tablespoons shredded Parmesan cheese, optional

1. Place flour and seasoned salt in large zip-top bag. Cut chicken into bite-size pieces and place in bag (wash hands).
2. Preheat large sauté pan on medium-high 2–3 minutes. Seal bag and shake to coat chicken. Add butter to pan; swirl to coat. Pour chicken, with flour, into pan; cook 4–5 minutes, stirring occasionally, or until chicken begins to brown.
3. Add broccoli to pan. Cover and cook 3 minutes, stirring occasionally. Stir in Alfredo sauce and wine; reduce heat to low. Cover and cook 2–3 minutes or until broccoli is desired tenderness. Serve topped with Parmesan cheese.

CALORIES (per 1/4 recipe) 353kcal; FAT 11g; CHOL 123mg; SODIUM 831mg; CARB 13g; FIBER 2g; PROTEIN 46g; VIT A 10%; VIT C 46%; CALC 15%; IRON 10%

aromatic rice

4–6 fresh chives (rinsed)

2 (8.8-ounce) pouches pre-cooked chicken-flavored rice

1 tablespoon butter

1. Snip chives finely using kitchen shears. Place all ingredients in microwave-safe bowl and cover.
2. Microwave on HIGH 3 minutes or until thoroughly heated. Stir and serve.

CALORIES (per 1/4 recipe) 116kcal; FAT 4g; CHOL 8mg; SODIUM 394mg; CARB 19g; FIBER 1g; PROTEIN 3g; VIT A 4%; VIT C 3%; CALC 1%; IRON 2%

Freeze leftover wine for future use. Wine will not freeze solid, so place in a zip-top freezer bag and then place the bag in a second zip-top freezer bag to prevent leakage.

shopping list

MEAT

1 1/2 lb boneless, skinless
  chicken breasts

PRODUCE

1 cup pre-diced onions
1 cup baby carrots
4 ounces pre-sliced baby
  portabella mushrooms
1 bag spring mix salad blend
  (5–7 oz)

DAIRY

1/4 cup shredded
  Parmesan cheese

DRY GROCERY

cooking spray
1 teaspoon Montreal
  steak seasoning
1 1/2 tablespoons
  balsamic vinegar
1/2 cup seasoned croutons
1/4 cup Caesar salad dressing

SUGGESTED ITEMS

mashed potatoes, Italian
  bread, cheesecake

balsamic chicken and vegetables with bistro salad

MEAL TIME: *20 minutes*

COOKING SEQUENCE

- Prepare chicken through step 2 - 10 minutes
- Prepare salad - 5 minutes
- Complete chicken and serve - 5 minutes

SERVES: *4*

SHORTCUT AND TIPS

Instead of spring mix salad blend, consider using any type of baby lettuce greens. There are many new mixes that will work well in this salad.

UTENSILS

large sauté pan with lid   salad bowl
microwave-safe bowl with lid   knife and cutting board
tongs, cooking spoon   measuring utensils

balsamic chicken and vegetables

1 cup pre-diced onions

1 cup baby carrots

4 ounces pre-sliced baby portabella mushrooms (rinsed)

1 1/2 lb boneless, skinless chicken breasts

cooking spray

1 teaspoon Montreal steak seasoning

1 1/2 tablespoons balsamic vinegar

1. Place onions, carrots, and mushrooms in microwave-safe bowl. Cover and microwave on HIGH 5 minutes or until hot.
2. Preheat large sauté pan on medium-high 2–3 minutes. Cut chicken into 1 1/2-inch-wide strips; coat with cooking spray. Add chicken to pan (wash hands); sprinkle with steak seasoning. Cover and cook 2–3 minutes, turning once, or until chicken begins to brown.
3. Drain vegetables and stir into chicken. Cover and cook 5 minutes, stirring once, or until vegetables begin to brown.
4. Remove lid and cook 3 more minutes, stirring once, or until vegetables are well browned. Stir in balsamic vinegar and serve.

CALORIES (per 1/4 recipe) 170kcal; FAT 1.5g; CHOL 65mg; SODIUM 270mg; CARB 9g; FIBER 2g; PROTEIN 28g; VIT A 100%; VIT C 10%; CALC 4%; IRON 6%

bistro salad

1 bag spring mix salad blend (5–7 oz)

1/2 cup seasoned croutons

1/4 cup shredded Parmesan cheese

1/4 cup Caesar salad dressing

1. Combine salad mix, croutons, and cheese in salad bowl.
2. Toss with dressing and serve.

CALORIES (per 1/4 recipe) 120kcal; FAT 11g; CHOL 5mg; SODIUM 310mg; CARB 4g; FIBER 1g; PROTEIN 3g; VIT A 35%; VIT C 10%; CALC 8%; IRON 4%

Clean mushrooms gently since the flavor of the mushrooms is in their delicate spores. Large mushrooms, such as portabellas, can be lightly brushed with cheesecloth or a paper towel. Use cleaned mushrooms immediately.

shopping list

MEAT

1 1/2 lb boneless, skinless
chicken breasts

PRODUCE

1/2 cup pre-sliced
green onions
2 teaspoons roasted garlic
8 ounces pre-sliced
fresh mushrooms
1 small green bell
pepper
8 ounces baby carrots
8 ounces fresh sugar
snap peas

DAIRY

1 tablespoon garlic butter

DRY GROCERY

1 tablespoon sesame oil
4 ounces sliced
water chestnuts
1/3 cup ponzu sauce
2 tablespoons molasses
2 (8.8-ounce) pouches pre-
cooked long grain rice
1/2 teaspoon seasoned salt

SUGGESTED ITEMS

White Mountain Bread,
cheesecake

chicken ponzu over rice with carrots and sugar snap peas

MEAL TIME: *35 minutes*

COOKING SEQUENCE

• Prepare chicken recipe through step 1 - 10 minutes
• Begin to microwave carrots and continue chicken through
  step 3 - 15 minutes
• Complete both recipes and serve - 10 minutes

SERVES: *4*

SHORTCUT AND TIPS

Ponzu is a Japanese sauce made with citrus juice and soy sauce. It is
served as a dipping sauce or used as a condiment.

UTENSILS AND COOKWARE

large sauté pan with lid   knife and cutting board
microwave-safe bowl with lid   measuring utensils
cooking spoons

chicken ponzu over rice

1 tablespoon sesame oil

2 teaspoons roasted garlic

1/2 cup pre-sliced green onions

8 ounces pre-sliced fresh mushrooms (rinsed)

1 small green bell pepper (rinsed)

1 1/2 lb boneless, skinless chicken breasts

1/4 teaspoon salt

1/8 teaspoon pepper

4 ounces sliced water chestnuts (drained)

1/3 cup ponzu sauce

2 tablespoons molasses

2 (8.8-ounce) pouches pre-cooked long grain rice

1. Preheat large sauté pan on medium-high 2–3 minutes. Place oil in pan; swirl to coat. Add garlic, green onions, and mushrooms. Cover and cook 3–4 minutes, stirring occasionally, or until mushrooms are browned.

2. Cut pepper and chicken into bite-size pieces (wash hands). Season chicken with salt and pepper. Move mushrooms to one side of pan; add chicken, peppers, and water chestnuts (wash hands). Cook 4 minutes, stirring occasionally, or until chicken is browned.

3. Stir in ponzu sauce and molasses; cook 3–4 minutes or until thoroughly heated.

4. Squeeze rice pouches to separate rice; tear corner to vent. Microwave on HIGH 2–3 minutes or until hot. Serve chicken over rice.

CALORIES (per 1/4 recipe) 500kcal; FAT 9g; CHOL 100mg; SODIUM 800mg; CARB 56g; FIBER 3g; PROTEIN 46g; VIT A 6%; VIT C 35%; CALC 10%; IRON 15%

carrots and sugar snap peas

8 ounces baby carrots

8 ounces fresh sugar snap peas (rinsed)

1 tablespoon garlic butter

1/2 teaspoon seasoned salt

1. Place carrots in microwave-safe bowl; cover and microwave on HIGH 5 minutes. Snip ends of peas, if needed.

2. Stir in remaining ingredients. Cover and microwave on HIGH 3–4 more minutes or until tender. Stir and serve.

CALORIES (per 1/4 recipe) 70kcal; FAT 3g; CHOL 5mg; SODIUM 280mg; CARB 8g; FIBER 1g; PROTEIN 1g; VIT A 180%; VIT C 10%; CALC 4%; IRON 2%

shopping list

MEAT

1 lb boneless chicken tenders

PRODUCE

4 ounces pre-sliced
  mushrooms
1/4 cup pre-diced red onions
1 bag fresh spring mix salad
  greens (4–5 oz)

DAIRY

1 tablespoon herb
  garlic butter

DRY GROCERY

1 1/2 tablespoons
  blackening seasoning
1/4 cup vermouth
1 (8.75-ounce) pouch
  pre-cooked long grain and
  wild (or brown) rice
cooking spray

SUGGESTED ITEMS

baby carrots, Italian bread,
  chocolate dessert

cajun-spiced tenders with field greens and rice

MEAL TIME: *20 minutes*

COOKING SEQUENCE
• Preheat grill; prepare rice and greens through step 2 - 10 minutes
• Prepare chicken, complete greens and rice; serve - 10 minutes

SERVES: *4*

SHORTCUT AND TIPS
Build this meal into a low-carb dinner salad by using the grilled chicken
over salad greens, topped with mushrooms and onions. Add salad
dressing and enjoy.

UTENSILS AND COOKWARE

2-sided tabletop grill   meat thermometer
large sauté pan with lid   measuring utensils
tongs, cooking spoon

cajun-spiced tenders

1 lb boneless chicken tenders

1 1/2 tablespoons blackening seasoning

cooking spray

1. Preheat 2-sided tabletop grill. Sprinkle all sides of chicken with seasoning (wash hands).
2. Coat grill with cooking spray. Place chicken on grill (wash hands). Close lid and grill 4–5 minutes or until internal temperature reaches 165°F. Use a meat thermometer to accurately ensure doneness. (If using regular grill, double cooking time, turning once.) Serve.

CALORIES (per 1/4 recipe) 120kcal; FAT 1.5g; CHOL 65mg; SODIUM 500mg; CARB 0g; FIBER 0g; PROTEIN 26g; VIT A 0%; VIT C 2%; CALC 2%; IRON 4%

field greens and rice

1 tablespoon herb garlic butter

4 ounces pre-sliced mushrooms (rinsed)

1/4 cup pre-diced red onions

1/4 cup vermouth

1 bag fresh spring mix salad greens (4–5 oz)

1 (8.75-ounce) pouch pre-cooked long grain and wild (or brown) rice

1. Preheat large sauté pan on medium-high 2–3 minutes.
2. Place garlic butter in pan; swirl to coat. Add mushrooms and onions; cook 3–4 minutes or until onions begin to brown.
3. Stir in vermouth, salad greens, and rice. Cover and cook 3 minutes, stirring often, or until rice is hot and greens are tender. Serve.

CALORIES (per 1/4 recipe) 140kcal; FAT 2g; CHOL 0mg; SODIUM 230mg; CARB 23g; FIBER 2g; PROTEIN 3g; VIT A 30%; VIT C 10%; CALC 4%; IRON 6%

Too hot, too cold, or just too much trouble to grill outdoors? Try using a grill pan. It should be heavy enough to provide fast, even heat distribution, with deep enough ridges to provide nice "grill" marks, and it is nice to have a quality nonstick interior coating to prevent sticking. Preheat the grill pan on your stovetop on medium-high. The cook time should be about the same as the noted regular grill time.

shopping list

MEAT

1 (10-ounce) package cooked
  southwestern chicken strips

PRODUCE

1/2 cup shredded lettuce

FROZEN

1/4 cup diced green
  bell peppers
1/4 cup diced onions

DAIRY

4 (10-inch) flour tortillas
1/2 cup shredded sharp
  Cheddar cheese

DRY GROCERY

1 (16-ounce) can refried
  beans with chiles
1/4 cup Buffalo wing sauce
1/4 cup canola oil
1 (15-ounce) can black beans
1/4 teaspoon chili powder
1/4 teaspoon ground cumin

SUGGESTED ITEMS

sour cream and salsa
  (for topping), Mexican rice,
  Key lime pie

buffalo chicken chimichangas with zesty black beans

MEAL TIME: *40 minutes*

COOKING SEQUENCE

- Prepare black beans and begin to cook - 5 minutes
- Prepare chimichangas and complete beans; serve - 35 minutes

SERVES: *4*

SHORTCUT AND TIPS

For extra flavor, add sliced black olives and jalapeño pepper slices to chicken mixture.

UTENSILS AND COOKWARE

large sauté pan
medium saucepan with lid
microwave-safe bowl

microwave-safe plate
  (may be paper)
cooking spoons, tongs
measuring utensils

buffalo chicken chimichangas

1 (10-ounce) package cooked southwestern chicken strips

1 cup refried beans with chiles

1/4 cup Buffalo wing sauce

4 (10-inch) flour tortillas

1/2 cup shredded sharp Cheddar cheese

1/2 cup shredded lettuce

1/4 cup canola oil

1. Tear chicken into bite-size pieces while placing in microwave-safe bowl. Stir in beans and wing sauce. Microwave on HIGH 2 minutes or until heated.

2. Place tortillas on microwave-safe plate (may be paper). Microwave on HIGH 30 seconds or until warm and softened. Mound 2 tablespoons of the cheese and 2 tablespoons of the lettuce in center of each tortilla. Stir chicken mixture, to blend sauce, and then divide evenly over top of cheese and lettuce.

3. Form tortilla into desired shape by folding right and left sides of tortilla, over mixture, just until edges meet (do not overlap). Starting with bottom edge, fold tortilla into thirds; once over mixture and then fold once more. Tortilla will be about 1 inch thick and 5 inches long.

4. Place oil in large sauté pan and preheat on medium-high 5–6 minutes. IMPORTANT NOTE: Stovetops may vary widely; oil should **not** reach smoke point, but should sizzle when tortilla is added. **Do not leave unattended.**

5. Place 2 chimichangas in pan, seam side down; cook 1–2 minutes on each side or until golden. Repeat. Serve with desired toppings.

CALORIES (per 1/4 recipe) 462kcal; FAT 23g; CHOL 70mg; SODIUM 1595mg; CARB 35g; FIBER 5g; PROTEIN 29g; VIT A 11%; VIT C 1%; CALC 12%; IRON 15%

zesty black beans

1 (15-ounce) can black beans (undrained)

3/4 cup refried beans with chiles

1/4 cup frozen diced green bell peppers

1/4 cup frozen diced onions

1/4 teaspoon chili powder

1/4 teaspoon ground cumin

pepper, to taste

1. Combine all ingredients in medium saucepan, stirring gently, until well blended. (Reserve remaining refried beans for chimichanga recipe.)

2. Cover and cook on medium 12–15 minutes, stirring occasionally, or until boiling.

3. Reduce to low; cook 10–15 more minutes to blend flavors. Serve.

CALORIES (per 1/4 recipe) 130kcal; FAT 1g; CHOL 0mg; SODIUM 600mg; CARB 21g; FIBER 8g; PROTEIN 8g; VIT A 2%; VIT C 8%; CALC 4%; IRON 15%

shopping list

MEAT

1 lb turkey tenderloins
  (or cutlets)

PRODUCE

3/4 cup orange juice

FROZEN

1 (11-ounce) box ripe
  plantains

DAIRY

3 tablespoons butter

DRY GROCERY

large zip-top bag
2 tablespoons flour
1 (5-gram) packet sazón
  with azafrán seasoning
2 tablespoons light
  brown sugar
1 1/2 cups orzo pasta
1 (19-ounce) can lentil soup
1/2 teaspoon chipotle
  pepper sauce

SUGGESTED ITEMS

sliced tomatoes, Cuban
  bread, guava pastries

turkey tenderloins and plantains with orzo and lentils

MEAL TIME: *30 minutes*

COOKING SEQUENCE

- Prepare orzo through step 3 - 10 minutes
- Prepare turkey; complete orzo and serve - 20 minutes

SERVES: *4*

SHORTCUT AND TIPS

To use fresh plantains, choose ripe ones with large dark areas on the skin and a soft center. Peel and cut into 1/2-inch-thick slices. Fry in a little butter 4–5 minutes on medium-high before using in this recipe.

UTENSILS AND COOKWARE

large sauté pan
medium saucepan with lid
microwave-safe plate
  (may be paper)

cooking spoons
knife and cutting board
measuring utensils

turkey tenderloins and plantains

2 tablespoons flour

1 (5-gram) packet sazón with azafrán seasoning

large zip-top bag

1 lb turkey tenderloins (or cutlets)

1 (11-ounce) box frozen ripe plantains

2 tablespoons butter

2 tablespoons light brown sugar

3/4 cup orange juice

1. Place flour and sazón seasoning in zip-top bag; shake to mix. Cut turkey into bite-size pieces; add to bag (wash hands). Seal tightly and shake to coat.
2. Preheat large sauté pan on medium-high 2–3 minutes. Place plantains on microwave-safe plate (may be paper); microwave on HIGH 2 minutes to thaw.
3. Place butter in pan; swirl to coat. Add turkey (wash hands); cook 3 minutes, stirring often, or until evenly browned.
4. Move turkey to outer edge of pan. Add plantains to center and cook 3 minutes, turning plantains often, to brown evenly.
5. Add brown sugar and orange juice; gently stir until blended. Bring to a boil.
6. Reduce heat to low; cook 3–5 minutes, stirring occasionally, or until sauce thickens.

CALORIES (per 1/4 recipe) 420kcal; FAT 14g; CHOL 85mg; SODIUM 290mg; CARB 45g; FIBER 0g; PROTEIN 30g; VIT A 15%; VIT C 35%; CALC 2%; IRON 15%

orzo and lentils

1 tablespoon butter

1 1/2 cups orzo pasta

1 (19-ounce) can lentil soup (undrained)

1 cup water

1/2 teaspoon chipotle pepper sauce

1/4 teaspoon salt

1/8 teaspoon pepper

1. Preheat medium saucepan on medium-high 2–3 minutes. Place butter in pan; swirl to coat. Add orzo and cook 2–3 minutes, stirring occasionally, or until lightly browned.
2. Stir in remaining ingredients. Cover and bring to a boil, stirring occasionally.
3. Reduce heat to low; cook 10 minutes, stirring occasionally, or until orzo is tender.
4. Remove from heat; let stand 5–8 minutes or until liquid is absorbed. Serve.

CALORIES (per 1/4 recipe) 330kcal; FAT 4.5g; CHOL 10mg; SODIUM 420mg; CARB 59g; FIBER 5g; PROTEIN 13g; VIT A 15%; VIT C 0%; CALC 4%; IRON 25%

shopping list

MEAT

1 lb turkey tenderloins
  (or cutlets)

PRODUCE

1 lb fresh asparagus spears
1 lemon (for juice)
1/2 cup grape tomatoes
1 bag romaine salad blend
  (8–10 oz)

DAIRY

1 (9-ounce) package
  refrigerated three-cheese
  tortellini
1 tablespoon garlic butter

DRY GROCERY

2 tablespoons
  quick-mixing flour
1 teaspoon seasoned salt
large zip-top bag
1 (15-ounce) jar Alfredo sauce
1/4 cup red wine vinaigrette
1/4 cup seasoned croutons

SUGGESTED ITEMS

crumbled blue cheese for
  salad, sourdough bread,
  lemon creme or pound cake

turkey asparagus sauté with tortellini and classic salad

MEAL TIME: *30 minutes*

COOKING SEQUENCE
• Prepare turkey through step 8 - 20 minutes
• Prepare salad; complete turkey and serve - 10 minutes

SERVES: *4*

SHORTCUT AND TIPS

To catch the seeds, squeeze the lemon into your hand, letting the juice run through your fingers into the sauté pan.

UTENSILS AND COOKWARE

large sauté pan with lid
large saucepan with lid
large salad bowl, tongs

colander, cooking spoon
knife and cutting board
measuring utensils

turkey asparagus sauté with tortellini

1 lb turkey tenderloins (or cutlets)

2 tablespoons quick-mixing flour

1 teaspoon seasoned salt

large zip-top bag

1 tablespoon garlic butter

1 lb fresh asparagus spears (rinsed)

1 (9-ounce) package refrigerated three-cheese tortellini

1 lemon (for juice, rinsed)

1 (15-ounce) jar Alfredo sauce

1. Fill large saucepan 1/2 full of water. Cover and bring to a boil on high for tortellini.
2. Cut turkey into bite-size pieces (wash hands). Preheat large sauté pan on medium-high 2–3 minutes.
3. Place flour and seasoned salt in zip-top bag and shake to mix. Add turkey (wash hands); seal tightly and shake to coat.
4. Place butter in pan; swirl to coat. Add turkey (wash hands); cook 3 minutes, stirring occasionally, to brown on all sides.
5. Wash cutting board with hot, soapy water. Cut 1 inch from tough root end of asparagus spears and discard. To do this quickly, group half the spears together, align ends, and slice with sharp knife. Cut into 2-inch pieces.
6. Stir tortellini into boiling water. Boil 7–9 minutes, stirring occasionally, or until tender.
7. Add asparagus to turkey; cover and cook 3 minutes, stirring occasionally, or until asparagus begins to lightly brown.
8. Squeeze juice of lemon into turkey. Stir in Alfredo sauce; reduce heat to low. Cover and cook 6–8 minutes, stirring occasionally, or until thoroughly heated.
9. Drain tortellini and return to pan. Stir turkey mixture into tortellini and serve.

CALORIES (per 1/4 recipe) 560kcal; FAT 25g; CHOL 160mg; SODIUM 1460mg; CARB 42g; FIBER 3g; PROTEIN 42g; VIT A 20%; VIT C 15%; CALC 20%; IRON 20%

classic salad

1 bag romaine salad blend (8–10 oz)

1/4 cup red wine vinaigrette

1/2 cup grape tomatoes (rinsed)

1/4 cup seasoned croutons

1. Place salad blend in salad bowl. Add dressing: toss to mix well.
2. Top with tomatoes and croutons. Serve.

CALORIES (per 1/4 recipe) 60kcal; FAT 3.5g; CHOL 0mg; SODIUM 260mg; CARB 6g; FIBER 1g; PROTEIN 2g; VIT A 40%; VIT C 25%; CALC 4%; IRON 4%

shopping list

MEAT

1 lb turkey tenderloins
  (or cutlets)

PRODUCE

1 lb steak-topper vegetables
  (fresh sliced mushrooms,
  onions, bell peppers)
4 fresh garlic cloves
1 tablespoon basil herb paste
1 (10-ounce) container
  pre-sliced zucchini and
  yellow squash (2 1/2 cups)
2 tablespoons pre-diced
  yellow onions

DAIRY

1 tablespoon butter
3 tablespoons shredded
  Parmesan cheese

DRY GROCERY

2 tablespoons extra-virgin
  olive oil
2 (8.8-ounce) pouches
  pre-cooked long grain rice
1 (26-ounce) jar tomato basil
  pasta sauce
1/2 teaspoon seasoned salt

SUGGESTED ITEMS

Caesar salad, French bread,
  layer cake

turkey cacciatore with rice and squash milanese

MEAL TIME: *20 minutes*

COOKING SEQUENCE
• Prepare turkey and begin to cook - 5 minutes
• Prepare squash, complete turkey and rice; serve - 15 minutes

SERVES: *4*

SHORTCUT AND TIPS
For a change of pace, serve Turkey Cacciatore over pasta or wild rice.

UTENSILS

large sauté pan with lid
microwave-safe bowl with lid
tongs, garlic press

cooking spoons
knife and cutting board
measuring utensils

turkey cacciatore with rice

1 lb turkey tenderloins (or cutlets)

2 tablespoons extra-virgin olive oil

1/2 teaspoon salt

1/4 teaspoon pepper

1 lb steak-topper vegetables (fresh sliced mushrooms, onions, bell peppers)

4 fresh garlic cloves

2 (8.8-ounce) pouches pre-cooked long grain rice

1 (26-ounce) jar tomato basil pasta sauce

1 tablespoon basil herb paste

2 tablespoons shredded Parmesan cheese

1. Preheat large sauté pan on medium-high 2–3 minutes. Cut turkey into bite-size pieces (wash hands).

2. Place oil in pan; swirl to coat. Add turkey (wash hands); season with salt and pepper. Add vegetables. Crush garlic, using garlic press, into pan. Use knife to remove garlic from bottom of press. Cook 8–10 minutes, stirring occasionally, or until turkey is browned and vegetables are tender.

3. Squeeze rice pouches to separate rice; tear corner to vent. Microwave on HIGH 2–3 minutes or until hot.

4. Reduce turkey to medium heat; stir in pasta sauce and basil paste. Sprinkle with Parmesan cheese. Cover and cook 2–3 minutes or until hot. Serve turkey over rice.

CALORIES (per 1/4 recipe) 520kcal; FAT 13g; CHOL 70mg; SODIUM 1040mg; CARB 62g; FIBER 5g; PROTEIN 37g; VIT A 35%; VIT C 290%; CALC 20%; IRON 20%

squash milanese

1 (10-ounce) container pre-sliced zucchini and yellow squash (2 1/2 cups)

2 tablespoons pre-diced yellow onions

1 tablespoon butter

1 tablespoon shredded Parmesan cheese

1/2 teaspoon seasoned salt

1. Place all ingredients in microwave-safe bowl; do not stir.

2. Cover and microwave on HIGH 6–7 minutes, stirring once, or until thoroughly heated. Stir and serve.

CALORIES (per 1/4 recipe) 40kcal; FAT 3g; CHOL 10mg; SODIUM 240mg; CARB 3g; FIBER 1g; PROTEIN 1g; VIT A 4%; VIT C 20%; CALC 2%; IRON 2%

superb seafood

mediterranean fish
over potatoes
(recipe on page 90)

nested crab cakes
with couscous
(recipe on page 106)

make a splash

From traditional dishes like batter-fried catfish to sophisticated selections such as scallops dijonnaise, the following pages offer you a tasty range of choices. And every bit as delightful as the flavors is the fact that these recipes are all so remarkably quick and easy to prepare. Even if you've never cooked seafood before, we promise that you'll be able to handle any one of these selections, and that you'll enjoy deliciously impressive results.

shopping list

SEAFOOD

1 1/2 lb salmon fillets
(skin removed)

PRODUCE

1 bag romaine salad blend
(8–10 oz)
8–10 fresh basil leaves
1 Bartlett pear
1 cup grape tomatoes
1/2 cup matchstick carrots

DAIRY

1/2 cup shredded
Parmesan cheese

DRY GROCERY

2 tablespoons dried
cherry-flavored cranberries
1/2 cup light Vidalia onion
salad dressing
1/2 teaspoon seasoned salt
1 tablespoon flour
large zip-top bag
2 tablespoons light
mayonnaise
1/4 cup chopped walnuts

SUGGESTED ITEMS

sourdough bread, cheesecake

parmesan-crusted salmon with crunchy pear salad

MEAL TIME: *30 minutes*

COOKING SEQUENCE
- Prepare salmon and begin to cook - 15 minutes
- Using clean knife and cutting board, prepare salad and serve - 15 minutes

SERVES: *4*

SHORTCUT AND TIPS

Most of the fat in this recipe (19g) comes from the salmon, a fat-rich fish, which is high in health-beneficial omega-3 fatty acids.

UTENSILS AND COOKWARE

large sauté pan with lid   knife and cutting board
salad bowl, tongs   measuring utensils
turning spatula

parmesan-crusted salmon

1/2 teaspoon seasoned salt

1 tablespoon flour

large zip-top bag

1 1/2 lb salmon fillets (skin removed; thawed, if needed)

2 tablespoons light mayonnaise, divided

1/2 cup shredded Parmesan cheese, divided

1. Combine seasoned salt and flour in zip-top bag. Cut salmon into 4 portions. Place in bag (wash hands); seal tightly and shake to coat.

2. Preheat large sauté pan on medium 2–3 minutes. Place fish on cutting board; spread 1 tablespoon of the mayonnaise over all 4 portions, to coat. Sprinkle 1/4 cup of the cheese over mayonnaise and press lightly until cheese sticks.

3. Place salmon in pan with cheese side down. Lightly coat fish with remaining 1 tablespoon mayonnaise and 1/4 cup cheese, pressing lightly until cheese sticks (wash hands). Cover and cook 5–6 minutes on each side or until internal temperature reaches 145°F (or flesh is opaque and separates easily with a fork). Serve.

CALORIES (per 1/4 recipe) 398kcal; FAT 25g; CHOL 118mg; SODIUM 525mg; CARB 2g; FIBER 0g; PROTEIN 40g; VIT A 4%; VIT C 11%; CALC 14%; IRON 4%

crunchy pear salad

1 bag romaine salad blend (8–10 oz)

1 Bartlett pear (rinsed)

8–10 fresh basil leaves (rinsed)

1 cup grape tomatoes (rinsed)

1/2 cup matchstick carrots

1/4 cup chopped walnuts

2 tablespoons dried cherry-flavored cranberries

1/2 cup light Vidalia onion salad dressing

1. Place salad blend in salad bowl. Slice pear into quarters; remove core and discard. Cut pear into bite-size pieces; add to salad.

2. Chop basil leaves finely (2 tablespoons); add to salad. Add remaining ingredients and toss well. Serve.

CALORIES (per 1/4 recipe) 199kcal; FAT 9g; CHOL 0mg; SODIUM 140mg; CARB 29g; FIBER 3g; PROTEIN 3g; VIT A 56%; VIT C 28%; CALC 3%; IRON 4%

Leftover cooked salmon makes a great salad. Just break the salmon into bite-size pieces and toss with fresh salad greens and Italian salad dressing.

shopping list

SEAFOOD

1 1/2 lb salmon fillets
  (skin removed)

PRODUCE

1/2 lb fresh pineapple chunks
1 lb fresh asparagus spears
1 cup refrigerated mild salsa

DAIRY

1 tablespoon garlic butter
2 teaspoons prepared
  horseradish

DRY GROCERY

1 tablespoon honey mustard
2 teaspoons cornstarch
cooking spray
1/2 teaspoon lemon
  pepper seasoning
2 cups instant rice
1/4 teaspoon seasoned salt

SUGGESTED ITEMS

French bread, fresh lemon
  wedges, fresh fruit

pineapple salsa salmon and rice with asparagus tips

MEAL TIME: *35 minutes*

COOKING SEQUENCE
• Prepare asparagus through step 1 - 5 minutes
• Prepare salmon through step 5 - 25 minutes
• Complete asparagus; complete salmon and serve - 5 minutes

SERVES: *4*

SHORTCUT AND TIPS
Try this recipe with peach salsa for a sweeter flavor.

UTENSILS AND COOKWARE

large sauté pan with lid   turning spatula
medium saucepan with lid   knife and cutting board
microwave-safe bowl with lid   measuring utensils
medium bowl, cooking spoons

pineapple salsa salmon and rice

1/2 lb fresh pineapple chunks

1 cup refrigerated mild salsa

1 tablespoon honey mustard

2 teaspoons cornstarch

2 teaspoons prepared horseradish

1 1/2 lb salmon fillets (skin removed; thawed, if needed)

cooking spray

1/2 teaspoon lemon pepper seasoning

1 1/2 cups water

2 cups instant rice

1. Chop pineapple into small pieces. Stir together, in medium bowl, with salsa, honey mustard, cornstarch, and horseradish; set aside.

2. Cut fish into 4 portions, if needed. Coat both sides of fish with cooking spray; sprinkle with lemon pepper seasoning (wash hands).

3. Preheat large sauté pan on medium-high 2–3 minutes. Place water in medium saucepan. Cover and bring to boil on high for rice.

4. Place fish in pan (wash hands); cook 3 minutes. Turn fish and add salsa mixture. Cover and reduce heat to medium; cook 5–7 minutes or until sauce thickens.

5. Meanwhile, stir rice into boiling water. Cover, remove from heat, and let stand 5 minutes. Fluff rice with fork; serve sauce over fish and rice.

CALORIES (per 1/4 recipe) 570kcal; FAT 19g; CHOL 100mg; SODIUM 720mg; CARB 57g; FIBER 4g; PROTEIN 40g; VIT A 15%; VIT C 50%; CALC 6%; IRON 35%

asparagus tips

1 lb fresh asparagus spears (rinsed)

1 tablespoon water

1/4 teaspoon seasoned salt

1 tablespoon garlic butter

1. Cut 1 inch from tough root end of asparagus spears and discard. To do this quickly, group half the spears together, align ends, and slice with sharp knife. Cut into 2-inch pieces. Place in microwave-safe bowl with water.

2. Cover and microwave on HIGH 4–5 minutes, stirring once, or until desired tenderness. Drain asparagus; stir in seasoned salt and garlic butter. Serve.

CALORIES (per 1/4 recipe) 50kcal; FAT 3g; CHOL 5mg; SODIUM 125mg; CARB 4g; FIBER 2g; PROTEIN 2g; VIT A 20%; VIT C 10%; CALC 2%; IRON 15%

shopping list

SEAFOOD

1 1/2 lb salmon fillets
(skin removed)

PRODUCE

1 bag fresh spinach leaves
(8–10 oz)

DAIRY

2 tablespoons shredded
Parmesan cheese (optional)
1 tablespoon butter

DRY GROCERY

1 (10-ounce) can diced
tomatoes with lime
juice/cilantro
1/2 cup light mayonnaise
2 (8.8-ounce) pouches
pre-cooked long and wild
grain (or brown) rice

SUGGESTED ITEMS

fresh salad blend, dinner rolls,
creme cake

santa fe salmon with fresh spinach wild rice

MEAL TIME: *15 minutes*

COOKING SEQUENCE
- Prepare salmon and begin to cook - 5 minutes
- Prepare rice and complete salmon; serve - 10 minutes

SERVES: *4*

SHORTCUT AND TIPS

If your family does not like wild grain or brown rice, you can substitute pre-cooked white rice instead.

UTENSILS AND COOKWARE

large sauté pan with lid
microwave-safe bowl with lid
medium bowl, tongs

cooking spoons
knife and cutting board
measuring utensils

santa fe salmon

1 1/2 lb salmon fillets (skin removed; thawed, if needed)

1/4 teaspoon salt

1/8 teaspoon pepper

1 (10-ounce) can diced tomatoes with lime juice/cilantro (well drained)

1/2 cup light mayonnaise

1. Cut salmon into 4 portions; season with salt and pepper (wash hands).
2. Preheat large sauté pan on medium-high 2–3 minutes. Combine tomatoes and mayonnaise in medium bowl.
3. Coat both sides of salmon with tomato mixture and place in sauté pan (wash hands); add remaining tomato mixture to pan. Cover and cook 3–5 minutes on each side or until internal temperature reaches 145°F (or flesh is opaque and separates easily with a fork). Cook time may vary depending on the thickness of the fish. Serve.

CALORIES (per 1/4 recipe) 420kcal; FAT 28g; CHOL 110mg; SODIUM 790mg; CARB 6g; FIBER 1g; PROTEIN 34g; VIT A 8%; VIT C 20%; CALC 4%; IRON 4%

fresh spinach wild rice

1 bag fresh spinach leaves (8–10 oz)

1 tablespoon butter

2 (8.8-ounce) pouches pre-cooked long and wild grain (or brown) rice

2 tablespoons shredded Parmesan cheese (optional)

1. Place spinach and butter in microwave-safe bowl. Cover and microwave on HIGH 3 minutes or until spinach begins to wilt.
2. Stir in rice and microwave on HIGH 4 more minutes or until thoroughly heated.
3. Let stand 2 minutes, fluff with fork, and then sprinkle with cheese. Serve.

CALORIES (per 1/4 recipe) 240kcal; FAT 6g; CHOL 10mg; SODIUM 490mg; CARB 38g; FIBER 2g; PROTEIN 6g; VIT A 140%; VIT C 35%; CALC 10%; IRON 15%

Having the Seafood department remove the skin from the fish fillets reduces prep time.

shopping list

SEAFOOD

1 1/2 lb snapper (tilapia or basa) fillets

PRODUCE

1 lb tropical fruit salad
(fresh pineapple,
strawberries, kiwi)
1 bag romaine salad blend
(8–10 oz)
1/4 cup pre-diced red onions
8–10 sprigs fresh cilantro
1 fresh garlic clove
1 avocado
1 1/2 cups grape tomatoes

DRY GROCERY

3 tablespoons
balsamic vinegar
1/2 teaspoon seasoned
pepper blend
2 tablespoons extra-virgin
olive oil
cooking spray

SUGGESTED ITEMS

sweet potatoes, corn muffins,
lemon pie

sautéed fish and tropical salsa with avocado and greens salad

MEAL TIME: *30 minutes*

COOKING SEQUENCE
• Prepare fruit salsa in fish recipe - 10 minutes
• Prepare salad - 10 minutes
• Complete fish and serve - 10 minutes

SERVES: *4*

SHORTCUT AND TIPS
Make the salsa a little sweeter by adding 1 tablespoon honey. Or include some fresh diced onions to add a balance of savory flavor.

UTENSILS AND COOKWARE

large sauté pan
medium bowl, salad bowl
whisk, tongs, cooking spoon

knife and cutting board
measuring utensils

sautéed fish and tropical salsa

1 lb tropical fruit salad (fresh pineapple, strawberries, kiwi)

1/2 cup grape tomatoes (rinsed)

8–10 sprigs fresh cilantro (rinsed)

1 tablespoon balsamic vinegar

1 1/2 lb snapper (tilapia or basa) fillets (thawed, if needed)

1/2 teaspoon seasoned pepper blend

cooking spray

1. Prepare salsa by cutting fruit into small pieces; cut tomatoes into halves or quarters. Place both in medium bowl. Chop cilantro finely (2 tablespoons); add to fruit. Stir in balsamic vinegar until blended.
2. Preheat large sauté pan on medium-high 2–3 minutes. Season both sides of fish with seasoned pepper. Remove pan from heat and coat with cooking spray. Add fish, with darker side up, to pan (wash hands); cook 2–3 minutes on each side or until internal temperature reaches 145°F (or flesh is opaque and separates easily with a fork). Serve fish with fruit salsa.

CALORIES (per 1/4 recipe) 230kcal; FAT 2.5g; CHOL 65mg; SODIUM 115mg; CARB 16g; FIBER 2g; PROTEIN 36g; VIT A 8%; VIT C 120%; CALC 8%; IRON 4%

avocado and greens salad

1 fresh garlic clove

2 tablespoons extra-virgin olive oil

2 tablespoons balsamic vinegar

1 bag romaine salad blend (8–10 oz)

1 cup grape tomatoes (rinsed)

1/4 cup pre-diced red onions

1 avocado (rinsed)

1. Cut garlic clove in half and rub the cut edges over inside of salad bowl (discard garlic). Add oil and vinegar; whisk until well blended.
2. Add salad blend, tomatoes, and onions. Cut avocado into quarters; then cut into bite-size pieces. Add to salad; toss well to blend. Serve.

CALORIES (per 1/4 recipe) 160kcal; FAT 12g; CHOL 0mg; SODIUM 20mg; CARB 11g; FIBER 4g; PROTEIN 2g; VIT A 25%; VIT C 30%; CALC 4%; IRON 4%

shopping list

SEAFOOD

1 1/2 lb tilapia (or basa) fillets

PRODUCE

5–6 sprigs fresh Italian parsley
1 lemon (for juice)
2 cups fresh broccoli florets

DAIRY

4 tablespoons butter

DRY GROCERY

4 teaspoons flour
1 teaspoon seasoned salt
large zip-top bag
1/4 cup white wine
8 ounces angel hair pasta
1/2 cup sun-dried
    tomato pesto

SUGGESTED ITEMS

fresh salad blend, dinner rolls,
    Bakery layer cake

tilapia with lemon butter sauce and angel hair fresca

MEAL TIME: *30 minutes*

COOKING SEQUENCE
- Put water on to boil for pasta; prepare tilapia and begin to sauté - 15 minutes
- Complete pasta and tilapia; serve - 15 minutes

SERVES: *4*

SHORTCUT AND TIPS

Fresh Italian, or flat-leaf, parsley adds a slightly peppery, fresh flavor to the lemon butter sauce.

UTENSILS AND COOKWARE

large sauté pan   cooking spoons
large saucepan with lid   knife and cutting board
spatula   measuring utensils
colander

tilapia with lemon butter sauce

1 teaspoon seasoned salt

4 teaspoons flour, divided

large zip-top bag

5–6 sprigs fresh Italian parsley (rinsed)

1 lemon (for juice, rinsed)

1 1/2 lb tilapia (or basa) fillets

3 tablespoons butter, divided

1/4 cup white wine

1. Place seasoned salt and 3 teaspoons of the flour in zip-top bag; shake to mix and set aside. Chop parsley leaves coarsely and measure (2 tablespoons); cut lemon in half. Set both aside.

2. Preheat large sauté pan on medium-high 2–3 minutes. Add fish to zip-top bag (wash hands); seal tightly and shake to coat.

3. Place 1 tablespoon of the butter in pan; swirl to coat. Add fish (wash hands); cook 3 minutes. Add 1 tablespoon of the butter to center of pan. Turn fillets, using spatula, distributing butter under each fillet. Cook 3 more minutes or until internal temperature reaches 145°F (or flesh is opaque and separates easily with a fork). Place fish on serving plates.

4. Place remaining 1 tablespoon butter and 1 teaspoon flour, wine, and juice of lemon in sauté pan. Heat 1–2 minutes, stirring occasionally, or until thickened. Stir parsley into butter sauce and serve over fish.

CALORIES (per 1/4 recipe) 249kcal; FAT 10g; CHOL 108mg; SODIUM 509mg; CARB 3g; FIBER <1g; PROTEIN 31g; VIT A 2%; VIT C 7%; CALC 0%; IRON 2%

angel hair fresca

8 ounces angel hair pasta

2 cups fresh broccoli florets (rinsed)

1 tablespoon butter

1/2 cup sun-dried tomato pesto

1. Fill large saucepan 1/2 full of water. Cover and bring to a boil on high for pasta.

2. Stir pasta into boiling water; boil 1 minute. Stir in broccoli; boil 4 more minutes, stirring occasionally, or until broccoli is desired tenderness.

3. Drain pasta mixture. Add butter to saucepan, using residual heat to melt butter. Stir in tomato pesto and pasta mixture; toss to mix and serve.

CALORIES (per 1/4 recipe) 303kcal; FAT 6g; CHOL 8mg; SODIUM 384mg; CARB 48g; FIBER 2g; PROTEIN 9g; VIT A 15%; VIT C 56%; CALC 2%; IRON 15%

shopping list

SEAFOOD
1 1/2 lb tilapia (cod, snapper, or sole) fillets

PRODUCE
1 lemon (for juice)
4 Bartlett pears
5–6 ounces fresh raspberries

FROZEN
1 (10.75-ounce) all-butter pound cake

DAIRY
2 cups refrigerated homestyle sliced potatoes
4 ounces prepared vanilla pudding
1/4 cup heavy whipping cream
1/4 cup crumbled tomato/basil feta cheese

DRY GROCERY
1 tablespoon extra-virgin olive oil
6 kalamata (or pitted black) olives
1 (14.5-ounce) can herb/garlic diced tomatoes
1 tablespoon sugar
2 (1-ounce) squares white baking chocolate

SUGGESTED ITEMS
fresh asparagus, sourdough bread

mediterranean fish over potatoes and pears anglaise

MEAL TIME: *40 minutes*

COOKING SEQUENCE
- Thaw pound cake, if needed
- Prepare dessert recipe through step 1 and begin to cook - 10 minutes
- Prepare fish recipe and serve - 20 minutes
- When ready to serve, complete dessert and serve - 10 minutes

SERVES: *4*

SHORTCUT AND TIPS
If you do not have an olive/cherry pitting tool, use a knife to cut the pit out of the olive.

UTENSILS AND COOKWARE
large sauté pan with lid
2 microwave-safe bowls
  (1 with lid)
colander, vegetable peeler

olive/cherry pitter
cooking spoons
knife and cutting board
measuring utensils

mediterranean fish over potatoes

1 tablespoon extra-virgin olive oil

2 cups refrigerated homestyle sliced potatoes

1/3 cup water

6 kalamata (or pitted black) olives

1/4 teaspoon salt

1/8 teaspoon pepper

1 1/2 lb tilapia (cod, snapper, or sole) fillets (thawed, if needed)

1 lemon (for juice, rinsed)

1 (14.5-ounce) can herb/garlic diced tomatoes

1/4 cup crumbled tomato/basil feta cheese

1. Place oil in large sauté pan; swirl to coat. Add potatoes and water; cover and cook on medium-high 5–6 minutes, stirring occasionally, or until potatoes are tender and water is absorbed. Meanwhile, remove pits from olives; chop olives coarsely.

2. Reduce heat to medium. Arrange potatoes evenly into a single layer; sprinkle with olives, salt, and pepper. Place fish (darker side up) on potatoes. Squeeze juice of one-half lemon over fish.

3. Drain tomatoes very thoroughly (press or squeeze tightly to remove as much liquid as possible). Spread tomatoes over fish and sprinkle with feta cheese. Cover and cook 4–6 minutes, without turning or stirring, or until internal temperature reaches 145°F (or flesh is opaque and separates easily with a fork).

4. Reduce heat to low; remove cover and cook 1–2 minutes to allow any extra liquid to evaporate. Serve.

CALORIES (per 1/4 recipe) 330kcal; FAT 10g; CHOL 95mg; SODIUM 1070mg; CARB 23g; FIBER 2g; PROTEIN 39g; VIT A 15%; VIT C 15%; CALC 10%; IRON 15%

pears anglaise

4 Bartlett pears (rinsed)

1 tablespoon sugar

2 (1-ounce) squares white baking chocolate

4 ounces prepared vanilla pudding

1/4 cup heavy whipping cream

1 (10.75-ounce) frozen all-butter pound cake, thawed

5–6 ounces fresh raspberries (rinsed)

1. Peel pears and remove core. Cut pears into bite-size pieces; place in microwave-safe bowl. Sprinkle with sugar; cover and microwave on HIGH 4 minutes or until tender. Let stand 5 minutes.

2. Place white chocolate, pudding, and cream in second microwave-safe bowl. Microwave on HIGH 2 minutes or until hot. Let stand 3 minutes; then stir until smooth and creamy. Meanwhile, cut pound cake evenly into six slices and place on dessert plates.

3. Just before serving, drain pears and spoon over cake slices. Pour sauce over pears; top with raspberries and serve. (Makes 6 servings.)

CALORIES (per 1/6 recipe) 410kcal; FAT 18g; CHOL 75mg; SODIUM 230mg; CARB 58g; FIBER 6g; PROTEIN 5g; VIT A 10%; VIT C 20%; CALC 6%; IRON 6%

shopping list

SEAFOOD

4 firm, white fish (mahi, snapper, or tilapia) fillets (1 1/2 lb)

PRODUCE

2 fresh garlic cloves
12 ounces fresh broccoli florets

DAIRY

1/2 cup lowfat buttermilk
2 1/2 tablespoons butter

DRY GROCERY

1 (2-ounce) package potato flakes (1/2 cup)
1/4 teaspoon lemon juice
1/2 teaspoon seasoned salt

SUGGESTED ITEMS

tartar sauce, cornbread, carrot cake

potato-crusted fish and fresh broccoli

MEAL TIME: *25 minutes*

COOKING SEQUENCE
- Prepare fish and begin to cook - 15 minutes
- Prepare broccoli and serve - 10 minutes

SERVES: *4*

SHORTCUT AND TIPS

Tartar sauce is suggested for the fish. However, in the Seafood department, you can find the latest trends in dipping sauces that would add a flavorful touch to this meal.

UTENSILS AND COOKWARE

large sauté pan
microwave-safe bowl with lid
shallow dish, plate
garlic press, spatula

cooking spoons
knife and cutting board
measuring utensils

potato-crusted fish

2 fresh garlic cloves

1/2 cup lowfat buttermilk

1/4 teaspoon salt

1/4 teaspoon pepper

4 firm, white fish (mahi, snapper, or tilapia) fillets (1 1/2 lb; thawed, if needed)

1 (2-ounce) package potato flakes (1/2 cup)

3 tablespoons butter, divided

1. Crush garlic cloves into shallow dish using garlic press. Use knife to remove garlic from bottom of press. Stir in buttermilk, salt, and pepper. Place fish in buttermilk mixture, turning to coat (wash hands); let stand 3–4 minutes.

2. Meanwhile, preheat large sauté pan on medium-high 3–4 minutes. Place potato flakes on plate. Coat both sides of fish with potato flakes; press with fingers to coat heavily. Place 2 tablespoons of the butter in pan; swirl to coat. Add fish (wash hands); cook 4 minutes. (Do not turn fish.)

3. Place remaining 1 tablespoon butter in center of pan. Turn fish, using spatula, distributing butter under each fillet. Cook 3 more minutes or until internal temperature reaches 145°F (or until golden and fish separates easily with a fork). Serve.

CALORIES (per 1/4 recipe) 290kcal; FAT 14g; CHOL 115mg; SODIUM 390mg; CARB 6g; FIBER 0g; PROTEIN 36g; VIT A 8%; VIT C 8%; CALC 8%; IRON 6%

fresh broccoli

12 ounces fresh broccoli florets (rinsed)

1/3 cup water

1/2 tablespoon butter

1/4 teaspoon lemon juice

1/2 teaspoon seasoned salt

1. Break broccoli into bite-size pieces, if preferred. Place in microwave-safe bowl with water. Cover and microwave on HIGH 4 minutes or until desired tenderness.

2. Drain; stir in remaining ingredients. Serve.

CALORIES (per 1/4 recipe) 35kcal; FAT 1.5g; CHOL 5mg; SODIUM 220mg; CARB 4g; FIBER 2g; PROTEIN 3g; VIT A 50%; VIT C 130%; CALC 4%; IRON 4%

shopping list

SEAFOOD
4 cod fillets or loins (1 1/4 lb)

PRODUCE
1 lemon (for juice)
1 bag fresh spinach leaves
    (8–10 oz)

BAKERY
2 tablespoons bread-dip
    seasoning (Sicilian blend)
1/2 teaspoon bread-dip
    seasoning (Parmesan blend)

DAIRY
2 tablespoons garlic butter

DRY GROCERY
1 (14.5-ounce) can
    diced tomatoes
1 (8.8-ounce) pouch
    pre-cooked long grain and
    wild (or brown) rice

SUGGESTED ITEMS
French bread, cherry
    cheesecake pie

monterey cod and rice with quick spinach

MEAL TIME: *15 minutes*

15 MINUTE
Meal Idea
Serve four in 15 minutes!

COOKING SEQUENCE
• Prepare fish through step 2 - 10 minutes
• Prepare spinach; complete fish and serve - 5 minutes

SERVES: *4*

SHORTCUT AND TIPS
Basa, tilapia, red snapper, or haddock will also work well in this recipe.

UTENSILS AND COOKWARE
large sauté pan with lid   meat thermometer
microwave-safe bowl with lid   knife and cutting board
cooking spoons, turning spatula   measuring utensils

monterey cod and rice

1 tablespoon garlic butter

4 cod fillets or loins
(1 1/4 lb; thawed, if needed)

2 tablespoons bread-dip
seasoning (Sicilian blend), divided

1 (14.5-ounce) can diced
tomatoes (well-drained)

1 lemon (for juice, rinsed)

1 (8.8-ounce) pouch
pre-cooked long grain and wild
(or brown) rice

1. Preheat large sauté pan on high 1–2 minutes; add butter. Sprinkle lightest side of fish with 1 tablespoon of the seasoning; place in pan with darkest side up. Sprinkle remaining 1 tablespoon seasoning over fish; cook 2 minutes, to brown. (Do not turn fish.)

2. Arrange tomatoes in pan around fish. Squeeze juice of lemon over fish; cover and reduce heat to medium-high. Cook 4–6 minutes or until internal temperature reaches 145°F (or flesh is opaque and separates easily with a fork). Remove fish from pan.

3. Reduce heat to medium and stir rice into tomato mixture. Cover and cook 1–2 minutes, stirring occasionally, or until thoroughly heated and liquid is absorbed. Serve.

CALORIES (per 1/4 recipe) 260kcal; FAT 3g; CHOL 55mg; SODIUM 1080mg;
CARB 26g; FIBER 2g; PROTEIN 29g; VIT A 10%; VIT C 60%; CALC 10%; IRON 10%

quick spinach

1 bag fresh spinach leaves
(8–10 oz)

1 tablespoon garlic butter

1/2 teaspoon bread-dip seasoning
(Parmesan blend)

1. Place spinach in microwave-safe bowl.

2. Cover and microwave on HIGH 4–5 minutes or until tender. Drain water from spinach, if necessary.

3. Stir in butter and seasoning. Serve.

CALORIES (per 1/4 recipe) 25kcal; FAT 1g; CHOL 0mg; SODIUM 110mg;
CARB 3g; FIBER 3g; PROTEIN 2g; VIT A 130%; VIT C 35%; CALC 8%; IRON 10%

shopping list

SEAFOOD

4 swordfish (or mahi) fillets
(1 1/2 lb)

PRODUCE

4 fresh garlic cloves
6–10 fresh basil leaves
1 large (or 2 medium)
tomatoes

DELI

1/2 cup artichoke and
spinach dip

DAIRY

1 (24-ounce) package
refrigerated mashed
potatoes

DRY GROCERY

1/3 cup slivered almonds
2 tablespoons extra-virgin
olive oil
1/2 cup roasted red peppers

SUGGESTED ITEMS

Italian bread, chocolate cake

swordfish romesco with artichoke spinach potatoes

MEAL TIME: *25 minutes*

COOKING SEQUENCE
- Prepare swordfish and begin to cook - 15 minutes
- Prepare potatoes and complete swordfish; serve - 10 minutes

SERVES: *4*

SHORTCUT AND TIPS

The artichoke and spinach dip makes a great topping for baked potatoes.

UTENSILS

large sauté pan   cooking spoon
food processor (or blender)   knife and cutting board
microwave-safe bowl with lid   measuring utensils
rubber spatula, tongs

swordfish romesco

1/3 cup slivered almonds

4 fresh garlic cloves

6–10 fresh basil leaves (rinsed)

2 tablespoons extra-virgin olive oil, divided

1 large (or 2 medium) tomatoes (rinsed)

1/2 cup roasted red peppers

4 swordfish (or mahi) fillets (1 1/2 lb; thawed, if needed)

1 teaspoon salt

1/2 teaspoon pepper

1. Place almonds, garlic, basil leaves, and 1 tablespoon of the olive oil in food processor (or blender); process until finely chopped. Cut tomatoes in half, remove stem and core; gently squeeze to remove seeds. Chop tomatoes coarsely and add to basil mixture with roasted red peppers. Process 30 seconds, scraping down side as needed, or until smooth.
2. Preheat large sauté pan 2–3 minutes on medium-high. Sprinkle both sides of fish with salt and pepper (wash hands). Place remaining 1 tablespoon olive oil in pan; swirl to coat. Add fish (wash hands); cook 3 minutes. (Do not turn.)
3. Reduce heat to medium and turn fish. Pour tomato sauce around fish; cook 5 more minutes or until internal temperature reaches 145°F (or flesh is opaque and separates easily with a fork) and sauce is thoroughly heated. Serve.

CALORIES (per 1/4 recipe) 350kcal; FAT 19g; CHOL 65mg; SODIUM 800mg; CARB 9g; FIBER 2g; PROTEIN 37g; VIT A 35%; VIT C 80%; CALC 4%; IRON 15%

artichoke spinach potatoes

1 (24-ounce) package refrigerated mashed potatoes

1/2 cup Deli artichoke and spinach dip

1. Combine both ingredients in microwave-safe bowl.
2. Cover and microwave on HIGH 3–4 minutes, stirring once, or until thoroughly heated. Stir and serve.

CALORIES (per 1/4 recipe) 300kcal; FAT 20g; CHOL 35mg; SODIUM 780mg; CARB 23g; FIBER 1g; PROTEIN 4g; VIT A 25%; VIT C 2%; CALC 10%; IRON 2%

Find peeled whole garlic cloves in the Produce department. No mess from peeling; they are ready for the garlic press.

shopping list

SEAFOOD
4 grouper fillets (1 1/2 lb)

PRODUCE
1 (1-ounce) package
   fresh basil
5–6 sprigs fresh Italian parsley
4 fresh garlic cloves

DAIRY
2 tablespoons butter

DRY GROCERY
2 tablespoons basil pesto
1/4 cup mayonnaise
1 teaspoon Dijon mustard
1 tablespoon Montreal
   steak seasoning
1 tablespoon extra-virgin
   olive oil
1 tablespoon capers
1 (26.5-ounce) box
   chopped tomatoes
8 ounces penne rigate pasta

SUGGESTED ITEMS
Parmesan cheese for
   pasta, fresh salad blend,
   Bakery dinner rolls,
   chocolate dessert

pesto grouper with
penne pasta pomodoro

MEAL TIME: *35 minutes*

COOKING SEQUENCE
• Preheat grill; put water on to boil for pasta
• Rinse and chop herbs for both recipes - 10 minutes
• Prepare pasta through step 4 - 15 minutes
• Prepare grouper; complete pasta and serve - 10 minutes

SERVES: *4*

SHORTCUT AND TIPS
All fresh herbs should be rinsed and patted dry. Chop as the recipe directs
and then measure. This gives the most accurate result and the best flavor.

UTENSILS AND COOKWARE

2-sided tabletop grill	cooking spoons
large saucepan with lid	meat thermometer
large sauté pan	knife and cutting board
medium bowl, colander	measuring utensils
garlic press, spatula	

pesto grouper

fresh basil leaves (about 3/4 cup, rinsed)

1/4 cup mayonnaise

1 teaspoon Dijon mustard

2 tablespoons basil pesto

4 grouper fillets (1 1/2 lb; thawed, if needed)

1 tablespoon Montreal steak seasoning

1. Preheat 2-sided tabletop grill. Chop basil leaves finely (1/2 cup); place in medium bowl. Stir in mayonnaise, mustard, and pesto until well blended.

2. Sprinkle both sides of fish with steak seasoning.

3. Coat fish with basil mixture and place on grill, topping with any remaining mixture (wash hands). Close lid and grill 5–7 minutes or until internal temperature reaches 145°F (or flesh is opaque and separates easily with a fork). Use a meat thermometer to accurately ensure doneness. (If using regular grill, double cooking time, turning once.) Serve.

CALORIES (per 1/4 recipe) 299kcal; FAT 16g; CHOL 73mg; SODIUM 742mg; CARB 2g; FIBER <1g; PROTEIN 34g; VIT A 5%; VIT C 0%; CALC 5%; IRON 9%

penne pasta pomodoro

10–15 fresh basil leaves (rinsed)

5–6 sprigs fresh Italian parsley (rinsed)

1 tablespoon extra-virgin olive oil

4 fresh garlic cloves

1 tablespoon capers

1 (26.5-ounce) box chopped tomatoes (well-drained)

1/2 teaspoon salt

1/4 teaspoon pepper

8 ounces penne rigate pasta

2 tablespoons butter

1. Fill large saucepan 1/2 full of water. Cover and bring to a boil on high for pasta. Chop basil (2 tablespoons) and parsley (1 tablespoon); measure and set aside.

2. Preheat large sauté pan on medium 2–3 minutes. Place oil in pan; swirl to coat. Crush garlic, using garlic press, into pan. Use knife to remove garlic from bottom of press.

3. Add capers, tomatoes, salt, and pepper. Reduce to low and cook 8–10 minutes, stirring often, or until flavors are well blended.

4. Stir pasta into boiling water. Boil 8–10 minutes, stirring occasionally, or until tender.

5. Stir herbs and butter into tomatoes. Cook 2 minutes, stirring occasionally, or until blended. Drain pasta thoroughly and stir into tomato mixture. Serve.

CALORIES (per 1/4 recipe) 328kcal; FAT 10g; CHOL 15mg; SODIUM 347mg; CARB 50g; FIBER 7g; PROTEIN 9g; VIT A 27%; VIT C 40%; CALC 1%; IRON 14%

Avoid rinsing cooked pasta. This decreases its ability to absorb the flavors from the sauce.

shopping list

SEAFOOD
1 1/2 lb boneless catfish fillets

PRODUCE
1 cup trinity mix (fresh diced onions, bell peppers, celery)

DRY GROCERY
1 (15.5-ounce) can black-eyed peas
1 cup canned Italian-style diced tomatoes
1 cup instant rice
2 tablespoons cooked bacon pieces
1/4 cup + 1 tablespoon canola oil
1 tablespoon hot pepper sauce
1 cup onion ring batter mix
1/2 cup flour

SUGGESTED ITEMS
cocktail or tartar sauce, coleslaw, cornbread, banana pudding

batter-fried catfish and hoppin' john

MEAL TIME: *35 minutes*

COOKING SEQUENCE
• Cut fish and chill - 5 minutes
• Prepare rice recipe and begin to bring to boil - 10 minutes
• Continue fish, complete rice recipe, and serve - 20 minutes

SERVES: *4*

SHORTCUT AND TIPS
For the best results, don't make batter in advance. Make it immediately before dipping the fish. Use sparkling water to make the batter even lighter and crispier.

UTENSILS AND COOKWARE
large sauté pan, turning spatula   cooking spoon
medium saucepan with lid   knife and cutting board
plate (may be paper)   measuring utensils
large bowl, whisk

batter-fried catfish

1 1/2 lb boneless catfish fillets (thawed, if needed)

1 cup onion ring batter mix

3/4 cup ice water

1 tablespoon hot pepper sauce

1/4 teaspoon pepper

1/2 cup flour

1/4 cup canola oil

1. Cut catfish into large chunks (about 2 inches square); chill until ready to cook (wash hands).
2. Whisk batter mix, water, pepper sauce, and pepper in large bowl until smooth and well blended; batter will be thick. Place flour on plate (may be paper).
3. Preheat large sauté pan on medium-high 3–4 minutes. Place oil in pan; swirl to coat. Dip catfish pieces in flour, lightly coating both sides, then shake off any excess. Dip into batter, turning to coat completely, and then allow excess to drip off.
4. Add half of the fish to pan (wash hands); fry 3–4 minutes on each side or until batter is crisp and golden. Place on paper towels to drain. Repeat with remaining fish; add a little more oil, if needed. Serve.

CALORIES (per 1/4 recipe) 510kcal; FAT 27g; CHOL 80mg; SODIUM 910mg; CARB 32g; FIBER 0g; PROTEIN 29g; VIT A 4%; VIT C 2%; CALC 2%; IRON 10%

hoppin' john

1 tablespoon canola oil

1 cup trinity mix (fresh diced onions, bell peppers, celery)

1 (15.5-ounce) can black-eyed peas (undrained)

1 cup canned Italian-style diced tomatoes (undrained)

2 tablespoons cooked bacon pieces

1 cup instant rice

1. Preheat medium saucepan on medium 2–3 minutes. Place oil in pan; swirl to coat. Add trinity mix and cook 2–3 minutes, stirring often, or until vegetables begin to soften.
2. Stir in remaining ingredients (except rice); bring to a boil, stirring occasionally.
3. Stir rice into boiling mixture; cover and remove from heat. Let stand (covered) 10–20 minutes or until rice is tender. Serve.

CALORIES (per 1/4 recipe) 260kcal; FAT 6g; CHOL 5mg; SODIUM 520mg; CARB 41g; FIBER 5g; PROTEIN 9g; VIT A 10%; VIT C 25%; CALC 6%; IRON 15%

shopping list

SEAFOOD

8 (5-ct) shrimp-on-a-skewer

PRODUCE

1/2 cup refrigerated ginger
  salad dressing
1 tablespoon roasted garlic
1 teaspoon chile pepper
  blend paste
2 large tomatoes
8–10 fresh basil leaves
1 large eggplant

DAIRY

2 tablespoons shredded
  Parmesan cheese

DRY GROCERY

2 tablespoons orange
  marmalade
1 tablespoon soy sauce
2 teaspoons sesame oil
1 teaspoon Chinese
  five-spice powder
2 teaspoons balsamic vinegar
1 1/2 teaspoons vegetable
  seasoning blend
olive oil cooking spray

SUGGESTED ITEMS

basmati rice, soft dinner rolls,
  lemon creme cake

garlic chile shrimp with grilled eggplant salad

MEAL TIME: *30 minutes*

COOKING SEQUENCE

- Preheat grill
- Prepare shrimp through step 2 - 10 minutes
- Prepare eggplant and begin to grill - 15 minutes
- Turn eggplant and add shrimp; complete grilling, assemble salad, and serve - 5 minutes

SERVES: *4*

SHORTCUT AND TIPS

Five-spice powder usually contains cinnamon, cloves, fennel seed, star anise, ginger, or peppercorns. Use in a stir-fry or to season poultry before roasting.

UTENSILS AND COOKWARE

grill, grilling tongs
medium saucepan
medium bowl

tongs, cooking spoons
knife and cutting board
measuring utensils

1/2 cup refrigerated ginger salad dressing

1 tablespoon roasted garlic

2 tablespoons orange marmalade

1 tablespoon soy sauce

1 teaspoon chile pepper blend paste

2 teaspoons sesame oil

8 (5-ct) shrimp-on-a-skewer (thawed, if needed)

1 teaspoon Chinese five-spice powder

garlic chile shrimp

1. Preheat grill. Combine dressing, garlic, marmalade, soy sauce, and chile pepper paste in medium saucepan. Allow sauce to cook on low, stirring occasionally, or until ready to serve (up to 20 minutes). Sauce should be hot and flavors well blended.

2. Meanwhile, drizzle oil over shrimp skewers; sprinkle with spice powder and let stand 5 minutes to marinate.

3. Place shrimp on grill (wash hands); cook 2 minutes. Turn shrimp and cook 1–3 more minutes or just until shrimp are pink and opaque. (Grills vary widely; adjust time as needed.) Serve shrimp with warm sauce on the side for dipping.

CALORIES (per 1/4 recipe) 200kcal; FAT 11g; CHOL 95mg; SODIUM 1000mg; CARB 10g; FIBER 0g; PROTEIN 15g; VIT A 8%; VIT C 8%; CALC 4%; IRON 10%

2 large tomatoes

8–10 fresh basil leaves

1 large eggplant

2 teaspoons balsamic vinegar

1 1/2 teaspoons vegetable seasoning blend, divided

olive oil cooking spray

2 tablespoons shredded Parmesan cheese

grilled eggplant salad

1. Preheat grill. Rinse tomatoes, basil, and eggplant. Cut tomatoes in half and remove stems and cores; gently squeeze to remove seeds. Chop tomatoes coarsely; place in medium bowl. Chop basil leaves (about 1 tablespoon). Stir into tomatoes with balsamic vinegar and 1/2 teaspoon of the vegetable seasoning; set aside.

2. Trim ends from eggplant and then cut lengthwise into 1/2-inch-thick slices. Coat both sides of slices with cooking spray and then sprinkle with remaining 1 teaspoon vegetable seasoning. Place eggplant slices on grill; cook 3–4 minutes on each side or until tender and golden.

3. Place eggplant slices on serving dish; top with tomato mixture. Sprinkle with cheese and serve.

CALORIES (per 1/4 recipe) 60kcal; FAT 1.5g; CHOL 0mg; SODIUM 230mg; CARB 12g; FIBER 6g; PROTEIN 3g; VIT A 15%; VIT C 25%; CALC 6%; IRON 4%

shopping list

SEAFOOD

1 lb large shrimp

PRODUCE

1–2 medium oranges (for
  juice and zest)
1–2 sprigs fresh rosemary
12 ounces fresh snipped
  green beans
1 cup pre-sliced baby
  portabella mushrooms

DAIRY

2 tablespoons prepared
  horseradish
1 (20-ounce) package
  refrigerated red
  potato wedges
1 tablespoon herb
  garlic butter

DRY GROCERY

1/4 cup light mayonnaise
2 tablespoons honey
1 1/2 teaspoons seasoned salt
3 tablespoons canola oil
1 tablespoon
  quick-mixing flour

SUGGESTED ITEMS

dinner rolls, carrot cake

sweet orange shrimp, oven herb potatoes, and beans with mushrooms

MEAL TIME: *45 minutes*

COOKING SEQUENCE

- Preheat oven; prepare potatoes (begin to bake) - 10 minutes
- Peel and devein shrimp, if needed - 15 minutes
- Prepare green beans and begin to microwave - 5 minutes
- Complete shrimp recipe, complete beans and serve - 15 minutes

SERVES: *4*

SHORTCUT AND TIPS

Purchase peeled/deveined shrimp to save 15 minutes of prep time.
Shrimp tails can be left on for extra color and flavor.

UTENSILS AND COOKWARE

large sauté pan
2-quart baking dish
microwave-safe bowl with lid
medium bowls, whisk
zester (or vegetable peeler)

kitchen shears
cooking spoons
knife and cutting board
measuring utensils

sweet orange shrimp

1 lb large shrimp (thawed, if needed)

1–2 medium oranges (for juice, rinsed)

1/4 cup light mayonnaise

2 tablespoons prepared horseradish

1 tablespoon honey

1 teaspoon seasoned salt

1 tablespoon canola oil

1 tablespoon quick-mixing flour

1. Peel and devein shrimp, if needed; wash hands.
2. Cut oranges in half; squeeze juice (1/2 cup) into medium bowl. Whisk in mayonnaise, horseradish, honey, and seasoned salt until blended; set aside.
3. Preheat large sauté pan on medium-high 2–3 minutes. Place oil in pan; swirl to coat. Add shrimp (wash hands); sprinkle with flour. Cook 2–3 minutes, stirring often, or until shrimp just begin to turn pink.
4. Stir in orange juice mixture; reduce heat to medium. Cook 3–4 minutes, stirring often, or until shrimp are pink and opaque and sauce thickens. Serve.

CALORIES (per 1/4 recipe) 240kcal; FAT 11g; CHOL 175mg; SODIUM 690mg; CARB 12g; FIBER 0g; PROTEIN 24g; VIT A 6%; VIT C 30%; CALC 6%; IRON 15%

oven herb potatoes

1–2 sprigs fresh rosemary (rinsed)

1 orange (for zest, rinsed)

2 tablespoons canola oil

1 tablespoon honey

1/2 teaspoon salt

1/8 teaspoon pepper

1 (20-ounce) package refrigerated red potato wedges

1. Preheat oven to 400°F. Snip rosemary, leaves only, using kitchen shears (1 tablespoon). Peel several strips of orange peel, without any white pith, with zester (or vegetable peeler). Chop finely for zest (1 tablespoon); place in medium bowl.
2. Add remaining ingredients (except potatoes); mix until well blended. Stir in potatoes until well coated; spoon mixture into 2-quart baking dish. Bake 30–35 minutes or until potatoes are tender and golden. Serve.

CALORIES (per 1/4 recipe) 170kcal; FAT 7g; CHOL 0mg; SODIUM 730mg; CARB 22g; FIBER 4g; PROTEIN 4g; VIT A 0%; VIT C 10%; CALC 0%; IRON 4%

beans with mushrooms

12 ounces fresh snipped green beans (rinsed)

1 cup pre-sliced baby portabella mushrooms (rinsed)

2 tablespoons water

1 tablespoon herb garlic butter

1/2 teaspoon seasoned salt

1. Place green beans, mushrooms, and water in microwave-safe bowl. Cover and microwave on HIGH 8–10 minutes or until beans reach desired tenderness. Drain, if needed.
2. Stir in remaining ingredients; cover and set aside 2 minutes. Stir and serve.

CALORIES (per 1/4 recipe) 40kcal; FAT 0.5g; CHOL 0mg; SODIUM 200mg; CARB 8g; FIBER 3g; PROTEIN 2g; VIT A 15%; VIT C 30%; CALC 4%; IRON 6%

shopping list

FROZEN SEAFOOD

4 lump crab cakes
(about 3/4 lb)

PRODUCE

4 medium or large pears
1 lemon (for zest)
2 fresh garlic cloves
1 bag fresh baby spinach
leaves (5–6 oz)

DAIRY

3/4 cup part-skim
ricotta cheese
1/4 cup crumbled
Gorgonzola cheese
1/4 cup whipped cream
cheese spread
1/4 cup + 1 tablespoon butter
1/2 cup aerosol whipped
cream (optional)

DRY GROCERY

1 (5.8-ounce) package
garlic/olive oil
(or seasoned) couscous
1/4 cup honey
2 tablespoons
cinnamon-sugar

SUGGESTED ITEMS

seafood dipping sauce,
fresh salad blend,
sourdough bread

nested crab cakes with couscous and pears with gorgonzola cream

MEAL TIME: *50 minutes*

COOKING SEQUENCE

- Prepare dessert through step 3; set aside - 25 minutes
- Prepare crab cake recipe and serve - 20 minutes
- Complete dessert when ready to serve - 5 minutes

SERVES: *4*

SHORTCUT AND TIPS

Add some sun-dried golden raisins to the pears as they cook for added sweetness.

UTENSILS AND COOKWARE

2 large sauté pans (1 with lid)   cooking spoons
microwave-safe bowl with lid   meat thermometer
medium bowl, whisk   knife and cutting board
zester (or vegetable peeler)   measuring utensils
spatula, garlic press

nested crab cakes with couscous

4 frozen lump crab cakes (about 3/4 lb)

1/4 cup butter, divided

1 1/4 cups water

1 (5.8-ounce) package garlic/olive oil (or seasoned) couscous

2 fresh garlic cloves

1 bag fresh baby spinach leaves (5–6 oz)

1/4 teaspoon salt

1/8 teaspoon pepper

1. Place crab cakes on microwave-safe plate; heat in microwave on DEFROST (30% power) 2 minutes or until thawed. Preheat large sauté pan on medium 2–3 minutes. Place 1 tablespoon of the butter in pan; swirl to coat. Add crab cakes gently; cook 5 minutes.

2. Add 1 tablespoon of the butter and turn crab cakes. Reduce heat to medium-low; cook 6 more minutes or until internal temperature reaches 165°F. Use a meat thermometer to accurately ensure doneness.

3. Meanwhile, combine water and 1 tablespoon of the butter in microwave-safe bowl. Cover and microwave on HIGH 3 minutes or until boiling. Stir in couscous mix; cover and let stand.

4. Remove crab cakes from pan and cover to keep warm. Add remaining 1 tablespoon butter to pan. Crush garlic, using garlic press, into pan. Use knife to remove garlic from bottom of press. Cook 1–2 minutes or until lightly browned. Add remaining ingredients; cover and cook 1–2 minutes, stirring occasionally, or until spinach is hot and tender. Form nests of spinach and top with crab cakes. Fluff couscous with fork and serve.

CALORIES (per 1/4 recipe) 420kcal; FAT 22g; CHOL 115mg; SODIUM 1169mg; CARB 39g; FIBER 3g; PROTEIN 18g; VIT A 51%; VIT C 15%; CALC 7%; IRON 11%

pears with gorgonzola cream

1 lemon for zest (rinsed)

3/4 cup part-skim ricotta cheese

1/4 cup crumbled Gorgonzola cheese

1/4 cup whipped cream cheese spread

1/4 cup honey

4 medium or large pears (rinsed)

1 tablespoon butter

2 tablespoons cinnamon-sugar

1/2 cup aerosol whipped cream (optional)

1. Peel a few strips of lemon peel, without any white pith, with zester (or vegetable peeler). Chop finely for zest (1 teaspoon). Place in medium bowl; add all cheeses and honey. Whisk 1–2 minutes or until smooth and well blended. Divide into serving bowls and chill until ready to serve.

2. Peel pears, remove cores, and cut into bite-size pieces.

3. Preheat large sauté pan on medium 2–3 minutes. Add butter; swirl to coat. Add pears and sprinkle with cinnamon-sugar; cover and cook 6–8 minutes, stirring occasionally, or until tender and browned. (Can be set aside until ready to serve.)

4. Spoon pears over cheese mixture; top with whipped cream and serve.

CALORIES (per 1/4 recipe) 403kcal; FAT 16g; CHOL 58mg; SODIUM 188mg; CARB 61g; FIBER 6g; PROTEIN 7g; VIT A 9%; VIT C 18%; CALC 17%; IRON 4%

shopping list

SEAFOOD

1 lb sea scallops

PRODUCE

2–3 green onions
2–3 sprigs fresh Italian parsley
12 ounces broccoli florets
1/2 cup matchstick carrots
1 lemon (for zest and juice)

DAIRY

2 tablespoons + 1 teaspoon
   butter
6 slices provolone cheese
3 tablespoons feta
   cheese crumbles

DRY GROCERY

2 cups instant rice
1/2 cup Alfredo sauce
1 tablespoon olive oil
1 tablespoon country
   Dijon mustard
1 1/2 teaspoons seasoned salt
2 tablespoons flour
large zip-top bag
1/4 cup semi-sweet white
   wine (Riesling)

SUGGESTED ITEMS

French bread, fruit pie
   or pastry

scallops dijonnaise, lemon rice, and feta broccoli

MEAL TIME: *40 minutes*

COOKING SEQUENCE

- Prepare broccoli through step 1 and rice through step 2 - 10 minutes
- Prepare scallops through step 3 - 15 minutes
- Complete rice, scallops, and broccoli; serve - 15 minutes

SERVES: *4*

SHORTCUT AND TIPS

Bay scallops may be substituted; however, you should reduce cook time in step 3 from 5 minutes down to 2 minutes.

UTENSILS AND COOKWARE

large sauté pan with lid
medium saucepan with lid
microwave-safe bowl with lid
zester (or vegetable peeler)

cooking spoons
knife and cutting board
measuring utensils

scallops dijonnaise

2–3 green onions (rinsed)

2–3 sprigs fresh Italian parsley (rinsed)

2 tablespoons flour

1/2 teaspoon seasoned salt

large zip-top bag

1 lb sea scallops (thawed, if needed)

2 tablespoons butter

1/4 cup semi-sweet white wine (Riesling)

1 tablespoon country Dijon mustard

1/2 cup Alfredo sauce

6 slices provolone cheese

1. Chop green onions and parsley finely; set both aside.
2. Preheat large sauté pan on medium-high 2–3 minutes. Combine flour and seasoned salt in zip-top bag; shake to mix. Pat scallops dry and add to bag (wash hands); seal tightly and shake to coat.
3. Place butter in pan; swirl to coat. Add scallops (wash hands); cook 5 minutes, stirring occasionally, or until lightly browned.
4. Stir in remaining ingredients (except cheese). Reduce heat to medium; cook 2 minutes, stirring occasionally, or until thoroughly heated.
5. Arrange cheese over scallops. Cover and reduce heat to low; cook 2–3 minutes or until cheese melts. Serve.

CALORIES (per 1/4 recipe) 390kcal; FAT 23g; CHOL 100mg; SODIUM 1090mg; CARB 10g; FIBER 0g; PROTEIN 32g; VIT A 20%; VIT C 10%; CALC 40%; IRON 6%

lemon rice

1 lemon (for zest and juice, rinsed)

1 1/2 cups water

1/2 teaspoon seasoned salt

1 teaspoon butter

2 cups instant rice

1. Peel several strips of lemon peel, without any white pith, with zester (or vegetable peeler). Chop finely for zest (1 tablespoon).
2. Squeeze juice of lemon (about 2 tablespoons) into medium saucepan. Add water, seasoned salt, and butter; cover and bring to boil on high.
3. Stir rice and lemon zest into boiling water; cover, remove from heat, and let stand 5 minutes. Serve.

CALORIES (per 1/4 recipe) 190kcal; FAT 1.5g; CHOL 5mg; SODIUM 200mg; CARB 40g; FIBER 1g; PROTEIN 4g; VIT A 0%; VIT C 10%; CALC 2%; IRON 15%

feta broccoli

12 ounces broccoli florets (rinsed)

1/2 cup matchstick carrots

3 tablespoons feta cheese crumbles

1 tablespoon olive oil

1/2 teaspoon seasoned salt

1. Cut broccoli into bite-size pieces, if preferred. Combine all ingredients in microwave-safe bowl.
2. Cover and microwave on HIGH 4 minutes or until desired tenderness. Stir and serve.

CALORIES (per 1/4 recipe) 80kcal; FAT 5g; CHOL 5mg; SODIUM 300mg; CARB 6g; FIBER 3g; PROTEIN 4g; VIT A 110%; VIT C 130%; CALC 8%; IRON 4%

weeknight wonders

chicken risotto soup
(recipe on page 138)

grilled fish tacos and rice
(recipe on page 114)

These selections are ideal for any night of the week, but they work especially well for those busy times when sitting down to a homecooked dinner seems next to impossible. In fact, some of these recipes take as little as 15 minutes to prepare. But we believe that everyone in your family will want to take the time to savor every single bite.

shopping list

MEAT

4 slices bacon

PRODUCE

4 large fresh basil leaves
1 bag fresh spinach leaves
   (8–10 oz)
2 cups fresh pre-sliced
   mushrooms
1 cup fresh pre-diced
   tomatoes
1 medium peach

BAKERY

1 baguette

FROZEN

1 lb cooked shrimp

DAIRY

2 ounces fresh
   mozzarella cheese

DRY GROCERY

2 tablespoons basil pesto
1/2 cup fat-free sun-dried
   tomato vinaigrette
1 tablespoon diced pimientos
1/2 teaspoon green
   pepper sauce
1/4 cup extra-virgin olive oil

SUGGESTED ITEMS

shredded cheese for salad,
   iced tea, Key lime pie

shrimp salad with warm bacon dressing and summer bruschetta

MEAL TIME: *25 minutes*

COOKING SEQUENCE

- Prepare bruschetta - 10 minutes
- Prepare salad and serve - 15 minutes

SERVES: *4*

SHORTCUT AND TIPS

If peaches are not in season, substitute fresh strawberries.

UTENSILS AND COOKWARE

microwave-safe bowl with lid
mixing bowls, salad bowl
cooking spoons

electric or serrated knife
knife and cutting board
measuring utensils

shrimp salad with warm bacon dressing

4 slices bacon

1 bag fresh spinach leaves (8–10 oz)

2 cups fresh pre-sliced mushrooms (rinsed)

1/2 cup fresh pre-diced tomatoes

1 lb frozen cooked shrimp (thawed)

1 medium peach (rinsed)

1/2 cup fat-free sun-dried tomato vinaigrette

1/2 teaspoon green pepper sauce

1. Cut bacon into bite-size pieces. Place in microwave-safe bowl (wash hands); cover and microwave on HIGH 3–4 minutes or until bacon is lightly crisp. Wash knife and cutting board with hot, soapy water.

2. Place spinach, mushrooms, tomatoes, and shrimp in salad bowl. Peel peach; discard peel and seed. Cut peach into bite-size pieces; add to salad bowl.

3. Stir vinaigrette and pepper sauce into bacon and drippings. Cover and microwave on HIGH 1 minute or until hot. Pour mixture over salad; toss well and serve.

CALORIES (per 1/4 recipe) 250kcal; FAT 4.5g; CHOL 230mg; SODIUM 740mg; CARB 24g; FIBER 3g; PROTEIN 30g; VIT A 150%; VIT C 50%; CALC 10%; IRON 30%

summer bruschetta

1 Bakery baguette

4 large fresh basil leaves (rinsed)

2 ounces fresh mozzarella cheese

1/2 cup fresh pre-diced tomatoes

1/4 cup extra-virgin olive oil

2 tablespoons basil pesto

1 tablespoon diced pimientos

1. Cut bread in half lengthwise, using an electric or serrated knife. Stack basil leaves and slice into thin strips; cut mozzarella into bite-size pieces. Set both aside.

2. Combine remaining ingredients in small bowl; spread onto bread halves. Top with mozzarella and basil. Slice bruschetta and serve.

CALORIES (per 1/4 recipe) 340kcal; FAT 20g; CHOL 10mg; SODIUM 500mg; CARB 33g; FIBER 2g; PROTEIN 8g; VIT A 8%; VIT C 10%; CALC 2%; IRON 10%

Slice the baguette quick and easily, without mashing the soft fresh center, by using an electric knife.

shopping list

SEAFOOD
4 mahi fillets (1 1/2 lb)

PRODUCE
1 lime (for juice)
1 1/3 cups pre-shredded
 cabbage
8–10 sprigs fresh cilantro

BAKERY
16 cinnamon-sugar raised
 doughnut holes

DELI
1/4 cup artichoke and
 spinach dip

DAIRY
1 tablespoon butter
1/4 cup sour cream
4 (10-inch) flour tortillas

DRY GROCERY
1 cup long grain white rice
1/2 teaspoon adobo
 seasoning (Spanish
 seasoned salt)
1/4 cup mild salsa
1/4 cup sliced black olives
2 tablespoons lemon curd

SUGGESTED ITEMS
fresh salad blend, sliced
 tomatoes

grilled fish tacos and rice with lemon cinnamon bites

MEAL TIME: *30 minutes*

COOKING SEQUENCE
- Preheat grill
- Prepare taco recipe through step 3 - 5 minutes
- Prepare dessert through step 1 - 5 minutes
- Complete tacos and rice; serve - 20 minutes
- Complete dessert when ready to serve

SERVES: *4*

SHORTCUT AND TIPS
Fish tacos are typically made with deep-fried fish, however this version uses grilled fish fillets such as mahi, tilapia, or swordfish.

UTENSILS AND COOKWARE
2-sided tabletop grill, tongs
medium saucepan with lid
2 microwave-safe plates
 (may be paper)

mixing bowls, whisk
cooking spoons
knife and cutting board
measuring utensils

grilled fish tacos and rice

2 cups water

1 tablespoon butter

4 mahi fillets
(1 1/2 lb; thawed, if needed)

1 lime (for juice, rinsed)

1/2 teaspoon adobo seasoning
(Spanish seasoned salt)

1 cup long grain white rice

8–10 sprigs fresh cilantro (rinsed)

1 1/3 cups pre-shredded cabbage

4 (10-inch) flour tortillas

1/4 cup Deli artichoke and
spinach dip

1/4 cup mild salsa

1/4 cup sliced black olives

1. Preheat 2-sided tabletop grill. Place water and butter in medium saucepan. Cover and bring to a boil on high for rice.
2. Cut fillets lengthwise into 1-inch-wide strips. Squeeze juice of one-half lime over fish; sprinkle both sides of fish with adobo (wash hands). Let stand 10 minutes to marinate.
3. Stir rice into boiling water. Cover, reduce to low, and let cook 20–25 minutes or until rice is tender and all water is absorbed (do not stir).
4. Remove large stems from cilantro and place leaves in medium bowl with cabbage. Squeeze juice of remaining one-half lime over cabbage and stir to coat; set aside.
5. Place fish on grill (wash hands); close lid and cook 3–4 minutes or until fish is opaque and separates easily with a fork. (Thickness of fish and grills may vary; adjust time as needed.)
6. Meanwhile, place tortillas on microwave-safe plate (may be paper) and cover with moistened paper towel. Microwave on HIGH 30–40 seconds or until tortillas are flexible and moist. Spread 1 tablespoon of the artichoke dip over each tortilla. Add fish strips down center of each tortilla. Top each with cabbage mixture, salsa, and sliced olives. Fold lower edge of tortilla up over filling, fold right side over filling, and then roll tightly. Fluff rice with fork and serve.

CALORIES (per 1/4 recipe) 610kcal; FAT 14g; CHOL 135mg; SODIUM 930mg; CARB 73g; FIBER 5g; PROTEIN 41g; VIT A 25%; VIT C 20%; CALC 15%; IRON 35%

lemon cinnamon bites

1/4 cup sour cream

2 tablespoons lemon curd

16 Bakery cinnamon-sugar raised
doughnut holes

1. Whisk sour cream and lemon curd together in small bowl until smooth. Chill until ready to serve.
2. Place doughnut holes on microwave-safe plate (may be paper) and microwave on HIGH 20–30 seconds or just until warm and soft (do not overheat). Drizzle sauce over doughnut holes or use as a dipping sauce. Serve.

CALORIES (per 1/4 recipe) 380kcal; FAT 24g; CHOL 35mg; SODIUM 310mg; CARB 38g; FIBER 1g; PROTEIN 3g; VIT A 2%; VIT C 0%; CALC 4%; IRON 6%

shopping list

MEAT

1 package fully cooked beef
roast (about 1 lb)

PRODUCE

1 pint grape tomatoes
3–4 sprigs fresh cilantro
1 lemon (for juice)

FROZEN

1 (10-ounce) box whole
kernel corn

DAIRY

4 (10-inch) flour tortillas
1 (24-ounce) package
refrigerated mashed
potatoes
2 cups shredded
Mexican-blend cheese
2 teaspoons prepared
horseradish

DRY GROCERY

1/4 cup Italian salad dressing
1 tablespoon + 1/4 teaspoon
green pepper sauce
1/4 cup fried peppers
and onions
1/4 cup mayonnaise
2 teaspoons country
Dijon mustard
1 teaspoon garlic powder
butter cooking spray

SUGGESTED ITEMS

salsa, refried beans with
chiles, Key lime pie

beef and potato quesadillas, tangy sauce, and tomato corn salad

MEAL TIME: *30 minutes*

COOKING SEQUENCE
- Prepare quesadillas and begin to cook - 15 minutes
- Prepare salad; prepare dipping sauce and serve - 20 minutes

SERVES: *4*

SHORTCUT AND TIPS

When in season, grilled fresh sweet corn adds a real southwestern touch to the salad recipe.

UTENSILS AND COOKWARE

large sauté pan
microwave-safe bowl
mixing bowls, colander

spatula, cooking spoons
knife and cutting board
measuring utensils

beef and potato quesadillas

1 package fully cooked beef roast (about 1 lb)

1 (24-ounce) package refrigerated mashed potatoes

1 teaspoon garlic powder

1/4 cup fried peppers and onions

1/8 teaspoon pepper

4 (10-inch) flour tortillas

2 cups shredded Mexican-blend cheese

butter cooking spray

1. Transfer roast to microwave-safe bowl. (Discard gravy.) Microwave on HIGH 1 minute or until softened.
2. Shred roast using two forks. Stir in potatoes, garlic, peppers and onions, and pepper. Microwave on HIGH 2 minutes or until thoroughly heated.
3. Divide meat mixture and place on one half of each tortilla, spreading to within 1/2 inch of edge.
4. Preheat large sauté pan on medium-high 2–3 minutes.
5. Sprinkle 1/2 cup cheese over filling. Fold tortilla in half and coat with cooking spray. Place 2 tortillas in pan, sprayed side down. Coat top with spray and cook 4–5 minutes on each side or until golden and crispy. Repeat. Serve with Tangy Sauce for dipping.

CALORIES (per 1/4 recipe) 820kcal; FAT 44g; CHOL 40mg; SODIUM 1872mg; CARB 59g; FIBER 5g; PROTEIN 44g; VIT A 26%; VIT C 49%; CALC 53%; IRON 21%

tangy sauce

1/4 cup mayonnaise

2 teaspoons prepared horseradish

2 teaspoons country Dijon mustard

1/4 teaspoon green pepper sauce

1. Combine all ingredients in small bowl.
2. Chill until ready to serve.

CALORIES (per 1/4 recipe) 113kcal; FAT 12g; CHOL 10mg; SODIUM 154mg; CARB 0g; FIBER 0g; PROTEIN 0g; VIT A 0%; VIT C 2%; CALC 0%; IRON 0%

tomato corn salad

3–4 sprigs fresh cilantro (rinsed)

1 pint grape tomatoes (rinsed)

1 lemon (for juice, rinsed)

1 (10-ounce) box frozen whole kernel corn

1/4 cup Italian salad dressing

1 tablespoon green pepper sauce

1. Chop cilantro finely (1 tablespoon); place in medium bowl.
2. Slice tomatoes in half and add to cilantro. Squeeze juice of one-half lemon over tomatoes.
3. Rinse corn in colander to thaw; drain well. Stir remaining ingredients into tomatoes. Chill 10 minutes or until ready to serve.

CALORIES (per 1/4 recipe) 139kcal; FAT 7g; CHOL 0mg; SODIUM 319mg; CARB 19g; FIBER 3g; PROTEIN 3g; VIT A 11%; VIT C 39%; CALC 2%; IRON 4%

Fried peppers and onions can usually be found on the shelf near roasted red peppers, close to pickles and olives.

shopping list

PRODUCE

1/2 cup sun-dried
   tomato spread
1/4 cup pre-diced
   fresh tomatoes
1/4 cup pre-diced green
   bell peppers
1/4 cup pre-diced red onions

BAKERY

1 baguette

DELI

1 lb fried chicken tenders

DAIRY

4 (1-ounce) slices
   provolone cheese

DRY GROCERY

1 (15.5-ounce) can red beans
1 (8.8-ounce) pouch
   pre-cooked long grain rice
1/3 cup light Caesar
   salad dressing
2 teaspoons red wine vinegar
1 tablespoon lime juice
butter cooking spray
1/2 cup pineapple preserves

SUGGESTED ITEMS

lemonade, layer cake

chicken tender panini and tomato chutney with confetti rice salad

MEAL TIME: *15 minutes*

15 MINUTE Meal Idea
Serve four in 15 minutes!

COOKING SEQUENCE

- Prepare panini; begin to grill - 10 minutes
- Prepare salad and serve - 5 minutes

SERVES: *4*

SHORTCUT AND TIPS

Roll chicken, shredded lettuce, and chutney in a flavored tortilla for a great wrap.

UTENSILS AND COOKWARE

2-sided tabletop grill
microwave-safe bowl with lid
large bowl

cooking spoons
serrated knife and cutting board
measuring utensils

chicken tender panini and tomato chutney

1/2 cup sun-dried tomato spread (from produce)

1/2 cup pineapple preserves

2 teaspoons red wine vinegar

1 Bakery baguette

4 (1-ounce) slices provolone cheese

1 lb Deli fried chicken tenders

butter cooking spray

1. Preheat 2-sided tabletop grill. Prepare chutney by combining tomato spread, preserves, and vinegar in microwave-safe bowl. Cover and microwave on HIGH 30 seconds to soften; mix until well blended.

2. Cut bread diagonally into eight long 1/2-inch-thick slices, using whole loaf except ends. Spread chutney on one side of each slice. Layer half of bread slices (chutney-side up) with cheese and chicken tenders. Top with remaining bread slices; gently compress sandwiches to flatten for grilling.

3. Coat grill with cooking spray. Place sandwiches on grill and press lid down firmly. Cook 5–6 minutes, occasionally pressing lid, or until crisp and golden. Slice sandwiches in half. Serve with extra chutney for dipping.

CALORIES (per 1/4 recipe) 831kcal; FAT 24g; CHOL 93mg; SODIUM 1381mg; CARB 74g; FIBER 1g; PROTEIN 40g; VIT A 4%; VIT C 0%; CALC 22%; IRON 48%

confetti rice salad

1 (8.8-ounce) pouch pre-cooked long grain rice

1 (15.5-ounce) can red beans (drained and rinsed)

1/4 cup pre-diced fresh tomatoes

1/4 cup pre-diced green bell peppers

1/4 cup pre-diced red onions

1/3 cup light Caesar salad dressing

1 tablespoon lime juice

1/2 teaspoon salt

1/8 teaspoon pepper

1. Squeeze rice pouch to break rice apart and tear opening to vent. Microwave on HIGH 1 minute or until rice is warm and tender.

2. Place rice in large bowl and stir in remaining ingredients. Serve (or chill up to 24 hours).

CALORIES (per 1/4 recipe) 230kcal; FAT 6g; CHOL 0mg; SODIUM 936mg; CARB 39g; FIBER 6g; PROTEIN 8g; VIT A 5%; VIT C 17%; CALC 4%; IRON 10%

shopping list

MEAT

4 (6-ounce) ground
   chuck patties
4 pre-cooked bacon slices

PRODUCE

4 ounces pre-sliced baby
   portabella mushrooms
1/4 cup pre-sliced
   green onions
1 tablespoon roasted garlic
2 medium tomatoes
1 bag American salad blend
   (lettuce, carrots, radishes;
   12 oz)

DAIRY

4 thin American cheese slices

DRY GROCERY

1 1/2 teaspoons seasoned
   pepper blend
4 wheat sandwich rolls
4 dill pickle slices
1/4 cup barbecue sauce
2 tablespoons mayonnaise
1/4 cup ranch salad dressing

SUGGESTED ITEMS

French fries and ketchup,
   baked beans, pecan pie

roadhouse burgers with blt salad

MEAL TIME: *20 minutes*

COOKING SEQUENCE

- Preheat grill
- Prepare salad through step 2 - 5 minutes
- Prepare burgers; complete salad and serve - 15 minutes

SERVES: *4*

SHORTCUT AND TIPS

Fresh avocado chunks would be a great addition to the BLT salad.

UTENSILS AND COOKWARE

grill, grilling spatula
microwave-safe bowl
microwave-safe plate
   (may be paper)
salad bowl, tongs

cooking spoon
meat thermometer
knife and cutting board
measuring utensils

roadhouse burgers

4 ounces pre-sliced baby portabella mushrooms (rinsed)

1/4 cup pre-sliced green onions

1 tablespoon roasted garlic

1 medium tomato (rinsed)

1 1/2 teaspoons seasoned pepper blend

4 (6-ounce) ground chuck patties

4 thin American cheese slices

4 wheat sandwich rolls

4 dill pickle slices

1/4 cup barbecue sauce

2 tablespoons mayonnaise

1. Preheat grill on medium-high. Combine mushrooms, green onions, and roasted garlic in microwave-safe bowl. Microwave on HIGH 1–2 minutes or until mushrooms are tender; set aside. Cut tomato into thin slices to top burgers (add any extra tomato to salad); set aside.

2. Sprinkle seasoned pepper over both sides of patties; place on grill (wash hands). Close lid (or cover with foil); grill 4–5 minutes on each side or until internal temperature reaches 155°F (for medium). During last 1–2 minutes of grill time, top each patty with 1/4 mushroom mixture and 1 cheese slice. Use a meat thermometer to accurately ensure doneness. (Grills vary widely; adjust time as needed.)

3. Place patties on bottom halves of rolls; top with pickles and tomato slices. Spread barbecue sauce and mayonnaise over top halves of rolls. Assemble and serve.

CALORIES (per 1/4 recipe) 754kcal; FAT 48g; CHOL 146mg; SODIUM 879mg; CARB 43g; FIBER 3g; PROTEIN 41g; VIT A 20%; VIT C 10%; CALC 26%; IRON 30%

blt salad

4 pre-cooked bacon slices

1 bag American salad blend (lettuce, carrots, radishes; 12 oz)

1 medium tomato (rinsed)

1/4 cup ranch salad dressing

1. Place bacon on microwave-safe plate (may be paper) and cover with paper towel. Microwave on HIGH 30–40 seconds or until crisp.

2. Place salad blend in salad bowl. Cut tomato into bite-size pieces; add to salad.

3. Crumble bacon over salad. Add dressing; toss to coat and serve.

CALORIES (per 1/4 recipe) 120kcal; FAT 10g; CHOL 10mg; SODIUM 270mg; CARB 5g; FIBER 1g; PROTEIN 4g; VIT A 30%; VIT C 30%; CALC 2%; IRON 4%

This meal can be served on disposable plates, making cleanup a snap.

shopping list

MEAT

1 package fully cooked beef
   roast (about 1 lb)

PRODUCE

3/4 cup pre-diced red onions
4 ounces pre-sliced baby
   portabella mushrooms
12 ounces fresh snipped
   green beans

BAKERY

4 slices Italian
   multigrain bread

DAIRY

3 tablespoons herb
   garlic butter
5 ounces extra-sharp
   Cheddar cheese
32 ounces refrigerated
   sour cream/chive
   mashed potatoes

DRY GROCERY

1/2 cup port or
   Burgundy wine
1/2 cup reduced-sodium
   beef broth
1 tablespoon cornstarch
1/4 cup regular (or Cheddar)
   French-fried onions
1 (14.5-ounce) can
   stewed tomatoes
1 tablespoon cooked
   bacon pieces

SUGGESTED ITEMS

fresh salad blend, fruit pie

mushroom beef melts, bistro potatoes, and tomato bacon beans

MEAL TIME: *35 minutes*

COOKING SEQUENCE

- Prepare beans and begin to cook - 5 minutes
- Prepare beef melts through step 2; continue beans - 15 minutes
- While beef sauce cooks, prepare potatoes through step 1 - 5 minutes
- Complete beef melts and potatoes; serve - 10 minutes

SERVES: *4*

SHORTCUT AND TIPS

For a "bistro-style" treat, shred extra cheese over the mashed potatoes before serving.

UTENSILS AND COOKWARE

large sauté pan
medium saucepan with lid
microwave-safe bowl with lid
small bowl, cooking spoons

rotary (or regular) cheese grater
knife and cutting board
measuring utensils

mushroom beef melts

1 tablespoon herb garlic butter

1/4 cup pre-diced red onions

4 ounces pre-sliced baby portabella mushrooms (rinsed)

1 package fully cooked beef roast (about 1 lb)

1/2 cup port or Burgundy wine

1/2 cup reduced-sodium beef broth

1/2 teaspoon pepper

1 tablespoon cornstarch

2 tablespoons water

4 slices Bakery multigrain bread

2 ounces extra-sharp Cheddar cheese

1. Preheat large sauté pan on medium-high 2–3 minutes. Place butter in pan; swirl to coat. Add onions and mushrooms; cook 3–4 minutes, stirring often, or until onions begin to brown. Meanwhile, cut roast into bite-size pieces; reserve sauce for next step.
2. Stir wine, broth, pepper, and (roast) sauce into onion mixture. Reduce heat to medium; cook 5–7 minutes, stirring often, or until liquid has reduced by half.
3. Combine cornstarch and water in small bowl until smooth. Slowly pour into sauce, stirring continuously, until blended. Bring sauce back to a boil, stirring often, or until sauce begins to thicken.
4. Reduce heat to low. Stir in roast; cook 1–2 minutes, stirring often, or until thoroughly heated. Place bread on serving plates; top with meat and sauce mixture. Grate cheese over top and serve.

CALORIES (per 1/4 recipe) 360kcal; FAT 15g; CHOL 85mg; SODIUM 760mg; CARB 21g; FIBER 1g; PROTEIN 31g; VIT A 4%; VIT C 4%; CALC 10%; IRON 35%

bistro potatoes

32 ounces refrigerated sour cream/chive mashed potatoes

3 ounces extra-sharp Cheddar cheese

1 tablespoon herb garlic butter

1/4 cup regular (or Cheddar) French-fried onions

1. Place potatoes in microwave-safe bowl; cover and microwave on HIGH 4 minutes or until partially heated.
2. Grate cheese finely. Stir into potatoes, with butter; microwave 3 minutes or until hot. Stir, top with fried onions, and serve. (Makes 6 servings.)

CALORIES (per 1/6 recipe) 260kcal; FAT 17g; CHOL 40mg; SODIUM 700mg; CARB 20g; FIBER 1g; PROTEIN 7g; VIT A 10%; VIT C 2%; CALC 15%; IRON 2%

tomato bacon beans

12 ounces fresh snipped green beans (rinsed)

2 cups water

1 (14.5-ounce) can stewed tomatoes (undrained)

1/2 cup pre-diced red onions

1 tablespoon cooked bacon pieces

1 tablespoon herb garlic butter

1/8 teaspoon pepper

1. Snap beans, if desired. Place in medium saucepan with water. Bring to boil on high; cook 7–10 minutes, stirring often, or until beans begin to soften.
2. Drain; stir in remaining ingredients. Reduce heat to low; cover and cook 10–12 minutes, stirring often, for crisp-tender (or until desired tenderness). Serve.

CALORIES (per 1/4 recipe) 130kcal; FAT 6g; CHOL 15mg; SODIUM 450mg; CARB 12g; FIBER 4g; PROTEIN 7g; VIT A 15%; VIT C 35%; CALC 6%; IRON 15%

shopping list

MEAT
1 3/4 lb boneless, skinless chicken thighs

PRODUCE
4–5 fresh chives

DAIRY
2 tablespoons crumbled blue cheese
1 (24-ounce) package refrigerated mashed potatoes

DRY GROCERY
large zip-top bag
2 teaspoons cooked bacon pieces
1/4 cup Buffalo wing sauce
1 tablespoon cornstarch
1 teaspoon seasoned salt
cooking spray

SUGGESTED ITEMS
celery sticks, coleslaw, garlic toast, Key lime pie

buffalo grilled chicken with blue cheese spuds

MEAL TIME: *15 minutes*

15 MINUTE Meal Idea
Serve four in 15 minutes!

COOKING SEQUENCE
- Prepare chicken and begin to grill - 5 minutes
- Prepare potatoes and complete chicken; serve - 10 minutes

SERVES: *4*

SHORTCUT AND TIPS
Prepare a dipping sauce for chicken with equal parts melted butter and Buffalo wing sauce.

UTENSILS AND COOKWARE
2-sided tabletop grill
microwave-safe bowl with lid
tongs, cooking spoon

meat thermometer
knife and cutting board
measuring utensils

1 tablespoon cornstarch

1 teaspoon seasoned salt

large zip-top bag

1 3/4 lb boneless, skinless chicken thighs

1/4 cup Buffalo wing sauce

cooking spray

buffalo grilled chicken

1. Preheat 2-sided tabletop grill. Place cornstarch and seasoned salt in zip-top bag; shake to mix. Add chicken and wash hands; seal tightly and shake to coat. Add wing sauce; seal tightly and knead bag to coat completely.

2. Spray both sides of grill with cooking spray. Place chicken on grill (wash hands); close lid and cook 8–10 minutes, pressing lid down occasionally to sear chicken. Cook until edges are crisp and internal temperature is 165°F. Use a meat thermometer to accurately ensure doneness. Serve.

CALORIES (per 1/4 recipe) 250kcal; FAT 8g; CHOL 165mg; SODIUM 940mg; CARB 3g; FIBER 0g; PROTEIN 39g; VIT A 15%; VIT C 15%; CALC 2%; IRON 10%

4–5 fresh chives (rinsed)

1 (24-ounce) package refrigerated mashed potatoes

2 tablespoons crumbled blue cheese

2 teaspoons cooked bacon pieces

blue cheese spuds

1. Chop chives finely and combine with remaining ingredients in microwave-safe bowl.

2. Cover and microwave on HIGH 4–5 minutes, stirring once. Stir and serve.

CALORIES (per 1/4 recipe) 247kcal; FAT 14g; CHOL 29mg; SODIUM 665mg; CARB 28g; FIBER 4g; PROTEIN 5g; VIT A 12%; VIT C 2%; CALC 4%; IRON 10%

Using the zip-top bag to season the chicken helps keep the cornstarch from ending up all over the counter.

shopping list

MEAT

1 lb boneless chicken cutlets

PRODUCE

16 ounces baby carrots
1 cup dried apple chips
32 ounces fresh tangerine
  juice (or orange juice blend)

FROZEN

1 (10-ounce) can strawberry
  daiquiri mixer

DAIRY

3 tablespoons butter

DRY GROCERY

1 tablespoon lime juice
1 cup corn flakes cereal
3/4 teaspoon seasoned salt
2 tablespoons flour
2 teaspoons cornstarch
2 tablespoons light
  brown sugar
2 tablespoons honey
large zip-top bag
2 tablespoons apple butter
  (or cinnamon applesauce)

SUGGESTED ITEMS

fresh fruit, ready-to-bake
  cookies

apple crisp chicken, honey carrots, and tangerine punch

MEAL TIME: *30 minutes*

COOKING SEQUENCE

- Prepare punch; prepare carrots through step 1 and set aside - 5 minutes
- Prepare chicken through step 1; begin to microwave carrots - 10 minutes
- Complete chicken and carrots; serve - 15 minutes

SERVES: *4*

SHORTCUT AND TIPS

The apple chips and corn flakes can be processed by using a zip-top bag. Seal tightly; crush mixture using a meat mallet (or rolling pin).

UTENSILS AND COOKWARE

food processor
large sauté pan
microwave-safe dish with lid
2 shallow bowls, pitcher

tongs, cooking spoons
meat thermometer
measuring utensils

apple crisp chicken

1 cup dried apple chips
1 cup corn flakes cereal
1/2 teaspoon seasoned salt
2 tablespoons flour, divided
1 lb boneless chicken cutlets
large zip-top bag
2 tablespoons apple butter
(or cinnamon applesauce)
2 tablespoons butter

1. Crush apple chips while adding to food processor; process until finely chopped. Add corn flakes, seasoned salt, and 1 tablespoon of the flour; process until coarsely chopped. Pour mixture into shallow bowl. Place remaining 1 tablespoon flour and chicken in zip-top bag; seal tightly and shake to coat (wash hands).
2. Preheat large sauté pan on medium 2–3 minutes. Place apple butter (or applesauce) in second shallow bowl; add chicken and turn to coat evenly (wash hands).
3. Add butter to pan; swirl to coat. Dredge chicken in corn flakes mixture and place in pan (wash hands); cook 3–5 minutes on each side or until internal temperature reaches 165°F. Use a meat thermometer to accurately ensure doneness. Serve.

CALORIES (per 1/4 recipe) 280kcal; FAT 10g; CHOL 80mg; SODIUM 370mg; CARB 20g; FIBER 1g; PROTEIN 27g; VIT A 8%; VIT C 15%; CALC 2%; IRON 15%

honey carrots

16 ounces baby carrots
2 tablespoons light brown sugar
1 tablespoon butter
2 tablespoons honey
2 teaspoons cornstarch
1/4 teaspoon seasoned salt

1. Combine all ingredients in microwave-safe dish.
2. Cover and cook on HIGH 10–12 minutes, stirring once, or until tender. Stir and serve.

CALORIES (per 1/4 recipe) 120kcal; FAT 3g; CHOL 10mg; SODIUM 210mg; CARB 24g; FIBER 2g; PROTEIN 1g; VIT A 310%; VIT C 15%; CALC 4%; IRON 6%

tangerine punch

32 ounces fresh tangerine juice
(or orange juice blend)
1 (10-ounce) can frozen
strawberry daiquiri mixer
2 cups water
1 tablespoon lime juice

1. Combine tangerine juice and strawberry mixer in pitcher.
2. Stir in water and lime juice; chill until ready to serve.

CALORIES (per 1/4 recipe) 280kcal; FAT 0g; CHOL 0mg; SODIUM 0mg; CARB 72g; FIBER 0g; PROTEIN 1g; VIT A 20%; VIT C 45%; CALC 0%; IRON 10%

shopping list

MEAT

1 (10-ounce) package
  refrigerated cooked
  chicken strips

PRODUCE

4 ounces pre-sliced
  mushrooms
2 green onions
3 ounces fresh spinach leaves
  (1 1/2 cups)
1 3/4 lb fruit salad (fresh cut
  melons, pineapple,
  strawberries)

DELI

2 tablespoons shredded
  Parmesan cheese, optional

FROZEN

3 ounces limeade concentrate
  (1/2 can)

DAIRY

1 (9-ounce) package
  refrigerated
  four-cheese ravioli
2 tablespoons butter

DRY GROCERY

1 tablespoon basil pesto
1/2 teaspoon poppy seeds
1/4 cup honey

SUGGESTED ITEMS

sliced tomatoes, Bakery
  multigrain bread

chicken ravioli florentine with lime-kissed fruit

MEAL TIME: *25 minutes*

COOKING SEQUENCE
- Prepare ravioli and begin to boil - 10 minutes
- Prepare fruit salad and chill - 10 minutes
- Complete ravioli and serve - 5 minutes

SERVES: *4*

SHORTCUT AND TIPS

Prepared basil pesto is a great time-saver in today's time-stressed kitchens. Stir a little into mayonnaise for a delicious sandwich spread or stir into a jar of pasta sauce to add flavor.

UTENSILS AND COOKWARE

large saucepan with lid   knife and cutting board
large bowl, whisk   measuring utensils
cooking spoons

chicken ravioli florentine

1 1/2 cups water

1 (9-ounce) package refrigerated four-cheese ravioli

4 ounces pre-sliced mushrooms (rinsed)

2 tablespoons butter

2 green onions (rinsed)

1 (10-ounce) package refrigerated cooked chicken strips

3 ounces fresh spinach leaves (1 1/2 cups)

1 tablespoon basil pesto

2 tablespoons shredded Parmesan cheese, optional

1. Combine water, ravioli, mushrooms, and butter in large saucepan. Cover and bring to boil on high. When boiling, remove lid and reduce heat to medium-high. Cook 8–10 minutes, stirring often, or until most of liquid is absorbed.

2. Chop green onions finely. Stir onions, chicken, spinach, and pesto into ravioli. Cook 2–3 minutes, stirring occasionally, or until spinach is tender. Sprinkle with Parmesan cheese and serve.

CALORIES (per 1/4 recipe) 370kcal; FAT 14g; CHOL 85mg; SODIUM 839mg; CARB 34g; FIBER 3g; PROTEIN 29g; VIT A 33%; VIT C 11%; CALC 14%; IRON 17%

lime-kissed fruit

1/4 cup honey

3 ounces frozen limeade concentrate (1/2 can), thawed

1/2 teaspoon poppy seeds

1 3/4 lb fruit salad (fresh cut melons, pineapple, strawberries)

1. Whisk honey, limeade, and poppy seeds together in large bowl.

2. Add fruit salad; toss to coat with dressing. Chill until ready to serve.

CALORIES (per 1/4 recipe) 125kcal; FAT <1g; CHOL 0mg; SODIUM 20mg; CARB 31g; FIBER 1g; PROTEIN 1g; VIT A 42%; VIT C 83%; CALC 2%; IRON 3%

Successful meal preparation by parent and child is rewarding and helps build relationships. Let the kids help. You'll be glad you did.

shopping list

MEAT
20 pepperoni slices

FROZEN
1 (24-ounce) package small
round ravioli

DAIRY
1 tablespoon butter
1 1/2 cups shredded
mozzarella cheese

DRY GROCERY
1 3/4 cups marinara sauce
6 (22g) crispy rice treat bars
6 (23g) fruit snack rolls
3 (23g) fruit twist snacks
(or gummy worms)

SUGGESTED ITEMS
fresh raw veggies with
ranch dipping sauce,
garlic bread, lemonade

skillet ravioli pizza with rainbow rolls (dessert "sushi")

MEAL TIME: *25 minutes*

COOKING SEQUENCE
- Prepare ravioli through step 1 - 5 minutes
- While ravioli cooks, let kids make dessert - 15 minutes
- Complete ravioli and serve - 5 minutes

SERVES: *6*

SHORTCUT AND TIPS
Make a new flavor next time. Top with ham and pineapple instead of pepperoni. Or add some black olives and Parmesan cheese.

UTENSILS AND COOKWARE

large sauté pan with lid   knife (may be plastic)
sushi dishes (optional)   measuring utensils
cooking spoon

skillet ravioli pizza

1 1/2 cups water

1 (24-ounce) package frozen small round ravioli

1 tablespoon butter

1 3/4 cups marinara sauce

1 1/2 cups shredded mozzarella cheese

20 pepperoni slices

1. Combine water, ravioli, and butter in large sauté pan. Cover and bring to boil on high.
2. Remove lid when boiling; reduce to medium-high. Cook 5–6 minutes, stirring often (to avoid pasta sticking), or until most of liquid is absorbed.
3. Stir marinara sauce into ravioli; reduce to low. Cook 2–3 minutes, stirring constantly, or until pasta is hot and tender.
4. Spread ravioli evenly into single layer. Sprinkle with cheese and arrange pepperoni slices over top. Cover and cook 3–4 minutes or until cheese melts.

CALORIES (per 1/6 recipe) 670kcal; FAT 32g; CHOL 100mg; SODIUM 1620mg; CARB 62g; FIBER 3g; PROTEIN 31g; VIT A 20%; VIT C 15%; CALC 45%; IRON 20%

rainbow rolls (dessert "sushi")

6 (23g) fruit snack rolls

3 (23g) fruit twist snacks (or gummy worms)

6 (22g) crispy rice treat bars

1. Remove packaging from all ingredients. Unroll fruit snack rolls and cut length in half (knife may be plastic). Lay two halves side by side (about 1/8 inch apart). "Curled" end of fruit roll will be starting edge for roll. (Place on paper plate for ease in cleanup.)
2. Cut fruit twists in half. Cut rice treat bars in half lengthwise. Place one fruit twist half down center of one rice treat half; top with remaining rice treat half and press together firmly. Lay rice treat across curled end of fruit strips.
3. Form "sushi" by rolling fruit roll strips very tightly into a cylinder (or cigar) shape around the rice treat. Cut across middle of each roll to create two pieces, trimming ends if needed, so treats will stand on edge and show cross-section of roll. Just for fun, serve on sushi dishes, if available.

CALORIES (per 1/6 recipe) 210kcal; FAT 3g; CHOL 0mg; SODIUM 180mg; CARB 43g; FIBER 0g; PROTEIN 2g; VIT A 4%; VIT C 40%; CALC 0%; IRON 2%

shopping list

MEAT

1 lb lean ground beef, 7% fat
(or ground turkey)

PRODUCE

2 teaspoons minced garlic
8 ounces classic salad blend
(iceberg lettuce, carrots,
red cabbage)
1 cup grape tomatoes
1 cup green seedless grapes
1/4 cup refrigerated poppy
seed dressing

DAIRY

1/2 cup shredded
Colby/Monterey Jack cheese

DRY GROCERY

1 cup whole kernel corn
1 (15.5-ounce) can
Sloppy Joe sauce
2 cups tri-color rotini pasta
2 tablespoons shelled
sunflower seeds

SUGGESTED ITEMS

Italian bread, brownies

sloppy joe rotini with pinball salad

MEAL TIME: *25 minutes*

COOKING SEQUENCE
• Prepare Sloppy Joe and begin final cook time - 15 minutes
• Prepare salad and serve - 10 minutes

SERVES: 6

SHORTCUT AND TIPS
The poppy seeds in the dressing add a nutty flavor to the sweetness of
the dressing. Tell your kids what kind of dressing it is *after* they have
tried it.

UTENSILS AND COOKWARE

large saucepan with lid	cooking spoon
salad bowl, tongs	measuring utensils

1 lb lean ground beef, 7% fat
(or ground turkey)

2 teaspoons minced garlic

1/2 teaspoon salt

1/8 teaspoon pepper

1 cup water

1 (15.5-ounce) can
Sloppy Joe sauce

1 cup whole kernel corn (drained)

2 cups tri-color rotini pasta

sloppy joe rotini

1. Preheat large saucepan on medium-high 2–3 minutes. Combine ground beef, garlic, salt, and pepper in saucepan. Cook 5–7 minutes, stirring to crumble meat, or until meat is brown and no pink remains.

2. Stir in remaining ingredients. Cover and bring to boil.

3. Reduce to medium and cook 8–10 minutes, stirring occasionally, or until pasta is tender. Serve.

CALORIES (per 1/6 recipe) 260kcal; FAT 6g; CHOL 45mg; SODIUM 740 mg;
CARB 31g; FIBER 3g; PROTEIN 21g; VIT A 10%; VIT C 8%; CALC 2%; IRON 50%

8 ounces classic salad blend
(iceberg lettuce, carrots,
red cabbage)

1 cup green seedless
grapes (rinsed)

1 cup grape tomatoes (rinsed)

2 tablespoons shelled
sunflower seeds

1/2 cup shredded Colby/Monterey
Jack cheese

1/4 cup refrigerated
poppy seed dressing

pinball salad

1. Place salad blend in salad bowl.

2. Add remaining ingredients; toss to coat and serve.

CALORIES (per 1/6 recipe) 130kcal; FAT 8g; CHOL 10mg; SODIUM 160mg;
CARB 11g; FIBER 1g; PROTEIN 3g; VIT A 20%; VIT C 15%; CALC 8%; IRON 2%

shopping list

MEAT
1 1/4 lb ground turkey

PRODUCE
8 ounces trinity mix (diced
   onions, bell peppers, celery)
1 tablespoon roasted garlic
1 teaspoon ginger spice paste

BAKERY
6 slices multigrain bread

DAIRY
1/2 cup light vegetable
   oil spread

DRY GROCERY
2 tablespoons vegetable oil
1 packet chili seasoning mix
   (about 1.25-ounce)
1 (16-ounce) can chili beans
1 (10-ounce) can milder diced
   tomatoes and green chiles
1 (8-ounce) can tomato sauce
1 tablespoon 10X
   confectioners' sugar
1 teaspoon ground cinnamon
1/4 teaspoon cayenne pepper

SUGGESTED ITEMS
shredded Cheddar cheese to
   top chili, fresh salad blend,
   Key lime pie

tasty turkey chili and ginger spice spread on multigrain bread

MEAL TIME: *25 minutes*

COOKING SEQUENCE
- Prepare chili and begin final cook time - 15 minutes
- Prepare spread recipe and serve - 10 minutes

SERVES: 6

SHORTCUT AND TIPS
Toasting the multigrain bread will enhance the rich taste of the oats, sunflower seeds, and whole wheat.

UTENSILS AND COOKWARE
large saucepan   cooking spoon
small bowl, whisk   measuring utensils

tasty turkey chili

2 tablespoons vegetable oil

8 ounces trinity mix (diced onions, bell peppers, celery)

1 tablespoon roasted garlic

1 1/4 lb ground turkey

1 packet chili seasoning mix (about 1.25-ounce)

1 (16-ounce) can chili beans (undrained)

1 (10-ounce) can milder diced tomatoes and green chiles (undrained)

1 (8-ounce) can tomato sauce

1. Preheat large saucepan on medium-high 2–3 minutes. Place oil in pan; swirl to coat. Add trinity mix and garlic; cook 6–8 minutes, stirring often, or until well browned.
2. Reduce heat to medium; add ground turkey (wash hands). Cook 5–7 minutes, stirring to crumble meat, or until meat is brown and no pink remains.
3. Stir in remaining ingredients. Bring to boil; reduce heat to low and cook 10–12 minutes, stirring occasionally, or until thoroughly heated and flavors are well blended.

CALORIES (per 1/6 recipe) 305kcal; FAT 13g; CHOL 75mg; SODIUM 945mg; CARB 22g; FIBER 7g; PROTEIN 22g; VIT A 24%; VIT C 29%; CALC 4%; IRON 17%

ginger spice spread on multigrain bread

1/2 cup light vegetable oil spread

1 tablespoon 10X confectioners' sugar

1 teaspoon ground cinnamon

1 teaspoon ginger spice paste

1/4 teaspoon cayenne pepper

6 slices Bakery multigrain bread

1. Combine all ingredients (except bread) in small bowl, using whisk, until well blended.
2. Spread mixture on bread and serve.

CALORIES (per 1/6 recipe) 96kcal; FAT 8g; CHOL 0mg; SODIUM 279mg; CARB 18g; FIBER 2g; PROTEIN 3g; VIT A 14%; VIT C 5%; CALC 1%; IRON 6%

shopping list

MEAT
3 slices salt pork (3 ounces)

PRODUCE
1 tablespoon roasted garlic
1/2 cup matchstick carrots
2 tablespoons pine nuts
1 bag romaine salad blend
(8–10 oz)

DELI/DAIRY
5 tablespoons grated
Romano cheese

FROZEN
1 (10-ounce) bag seasoning
blend (diced onions, bell
peppers, celery)
1 (16-ounce) loaf garlic bread

DRY GROCERY
1 tablespoon olive oil
2 teaspoons Italian seasoning
1 (32-ounce) box reduced-
sodium chicken broth
2 (15.8-ounce) cans great
Northern beans
1/4 cup sun-dried
tomato pesto
1 cup ditalini pasta
1/3 cup Caesar salad dressing
1/2 cup seasoned croutons

SUGGESTED ITEMS
melon-wrapped prosciutto
or cheese and salami on
crackers (for appetizer),
tiramisu

pasta fagioli, romano bread, and caesar salad

MEAL TIME: *35 minutes*

COOKING SEQUENCE
- Prepare bread through step 2 - 5 minutes
- Prepare soup through step 3 - 15 minutes
- Complete bread and soup; prepare salad and serve - 15 minutes

SERVES: *4*

SHORTCUT AND TIPS
Use a clean knife/cutting board, for slicing bread, to avoid cross-
contamination from raw meat.

UTENSILS AND COOKWARE

large saucepan with lid
baking sheet, salad bowl
tongs, cooking spoon

knife and cutting board
measuring utensils

3 slices salt pork (3 ounces)

1 tablespoon olive oil

1 tablespoon roasted garlic

1 (10-ounce) bag frozen seasoning blend (diced onions, bell peppers, celery)

1/2 cup matchstick carrots

1 teaspoon Italian seasoning

1/4 teaspoon cracked black pepper

1 (32-ounce) box reduced-sodium chicken broth

2 (15.8-ounce) cans great Northern beans (undrained)

1/4 cup sun-dried tomato pesto

1 cup ditalini pasta

pasta fagioli

1. Cut salt pork into small pieces. Preheat large saucepan on medium-high 2–3 minutes. Place olive oil in pan; swirl to coat. Add salt pork; cook 2 minutes, stirring often, or until salt pork begins to melt.

2. Stir in garlic and seasoning blend; cook 4 minutes, stirring often, or until browned.

3. Stir in remaining ingredients (except pasta); cover and bring to boil.

4. Stir in pasta; cover and return to boil. Remove lid; reduce heat to medium and cook 8–10 minutes or until pasta is tender. Serve. (Makes 6 servings.)

CALORIES (per 1/6 recipe) 370kcal; FAT 16g; CHOL 15mg; SODIUM 860mg; CARB 41g; FIBER 9g; PROTEIN 14g; VIT A 40%; VIT C 4%; CALC 6%; IRON 15%

1 (16-ounce) loaf frozen garlic bread

2 tablespoons pine nuts

1 tablespoon grated Romano cheese

1 teaspoon Italian seasoning

romano bread

1. Preheat oven to 400°F. Arrange bread halves (butter side up) on baking sheet.

2. Chop pine nuts finely; sprinkle over bread with cheese and seasoning.

3. Bake 12–15 minutes or until golden. Slice and serve. (Makes 6 servings.)

CALORIES (per 1/6 recipe) 180kcal; FAT 8g; CHOL 0mg; SODIUM 210mg; CARB 22g; FIBER 1g; PROTEIN 5g; VIT A 2%; VIT C 0%; CALC 2%; IRON 4%

1 bag romaine salad blend (8–10 oz)

1/3 cup Caesar salad dressing

1/2 cup seasoned croutons

1/4 cup grated Romano cheese

caesar salad

1. Place salad blend in salad bowl.

2. Add remaining ingredients; toss and serve.

CALORIES (per 1/4 recipe) 170kcal; FAT 15g; CHOL 10mg; SODIUM 410mg; CARB 6g; FIBER 2g; PROTEIN 5g; VIT A 80%; VIT C 30%; CALC 10%; IRON 4%

shopping list

MEAT

10 ounces cooked chicken
(or turkey)

PRODUCE

3 ounces fresh spinach leaves
(1 1/2 cups)
15–20 fresh chives
8 ounces trinity mix (diced
onions, bell peppers, celery)
8 ounces pre-sliced baby
portabella mushrooms
5 fresh garlic cloves

BAKERY

12 potato dinner rolls

DAIRY

3/4 cup half-and-half
2 tablespoons butter
1 1/2 tablespoons reduced-fat
sour cream

DRY GROCERY

1 (32-ounce) box
chicken broth
1/3 cup long grain white rice
1 tablespoon extra-virgin
olive oil
2 tablespoons cornstarch
1/3 cup white wine

SUGGESTED ITEMS

fresh salad blend, fruit pie
or pastry

chicken risotto soup and chive butter rolls

MEAL TIME: *40 minutes*

COOKING SEQUENCE
- Preheat oven; prepare soup through step 3 - 20 minutes
- While soup cooks, prepare rolls and begin to bake - 10 minutes
- Complete soup and serve - 10 minutes

SERVES: 6

SHORTCUT AND TIPS
This recipe would be delicious made with leftover rotisserie chicken or roasted turkey.

UTENSILS AND COOKWARE

large saucepan, baking sheet   cooking spoons
microwave-safe bowl   knife and cutting board
small bowl, garlic press   measuring utensils

chicken risotto soup

1 tablespoon extra-virgin olive oil

8 ounces trinity mix (fresh diced onions, bell peppers, celery)

8 ounces pre-sliced baby portabella mushrooms (rinsed)

1/2 teaspoon pepper

5 fresh garlic cloves

3 ounces fresh spinach leaves (1 1/2 cups)

1/3 cup long grain white rice

1 (32-ounce) box chicken broth

3/4 cup half-and-half

1/3 cup white wine

10 ounces cooked chicken (or turkey)

1/4 cup water

2 tablespoons cornstarch

1. Preheat large saucepan on medium-high 2–3 minutes. Place olive oil in pan; swirl to coat. Add trinity mix, mushrooms, and pepper. Crush garlic into pan using garlic press. Use knife to remove garlic from bottom of press. Cook 3–4 minutes, stirring often, or until vegetables begin to brown. Meanwhile, chop spinach coarsely.

2. Stir in rice and spinach. Cook 1–2 minutes, stirring often, until spinach wilts. Stir in broth, half-and-half, and wine (in that order); bring to boil.

3. Reduce heat to medium; cook 15–17 minutes, stirring occasionally, or until rice is tender. Meanwhile, cut chicken into bite-size pieces; set aside.

4. Combine water and cornstarch in small bowl until well blended. Stir chicken into soup. Slowly add cornstarch mixture, stirring continuously, or until blended and soup begins to thicken. Cook 2–3 more minutes, stirring occasionally, to heat chicken and blend flavors. Serve.

CALORIES (per 1/6 recipe) 250kcal; FAT 11g; CHOL 50mg; SODIUM 990mg; CARB 21g; FIBER 2g; PROTEIN 15g; VIT A 30%; VIT C 25%; CALC 6%; IRON 8%

chive butter rolls

12 Bakery potato dinner rolls

15–20 fresh chives (rinsed)

1 1/2 tablespoons reduced-fat sour cream

2 tablespoons butter

1. Preheat oven to 350°F. Arrange rolls on baking sheet.

2. Chop chives finely (2 tablespoons); place in microwave-safe bowl with sour cream and butter. Microwave on HIGH 20–30 seconds or until butter melts. Stir mixture and spoon over rolls. Bake 10–15 minutes or until golden and heated. Serve.

CALORIES (per 1/6 recipe) 240kcal; FAT 9g; CHOL 10mg; SODIUM 250mg; CARB 30g; FIBER 2g; PROTEIN 4g; VIT A 4%; VIT C 10%; CALC 0%; IRON 8%

Select a good quality garlic press. The best one we found is easy to grip (even with one hand), is odor resistant with a nonstick coating, comes with a self-storing (so you won't lose it) cleaning tool, and is dishwasher safe.

shopping list

PRODUCE
1/4 cup matchstick carrots

DELI
1 (16-ounce) container
  old-fashioned beans
1 lemon pepper
  rotisserie chicken

DAIRY
1 tablespoon butter

DRY GROCERY
1 (15-ounce) can black beans
1 tablespoon honey
1 tablespoon mustard
1/4 cup dried cherry-flavored
  cranberries
2 cups homestyle herb
  stuffing mix
1 (8.8-ounce) package pre-
  cooked long grain and wild
  (or brown) rice
aluminum foil

SUGGESTED ITEMS
fresh salad blend, French
  bread, creme cake

deli rotisserie chicken with rice stuffing and two-bean medley

MEAL TIME: *15 minutes*

15 MINUTE
Meal Idea
Serve four in 15 minutes!

COOKING SEQUENCE
- Prepare chicken and stuffing recipe through beginning of stand time - 8 minutes
- Prepare beans, stir stuffing and serve - 7 minutes

SERVES: *4*

SHORTCUT AND TIPS
Add 1/4 cup toasted chopped walnuts to the stuffing for crunch and flavor.

UTENSILS AND COOKWARE
large saucepan with lid   cooking spoons
baking pan   measuring utensils
microwave-safe bowl with lid

deli rotisserie chicken with rice stuffing

1 Deli lemon pepper rotisserie chicken

aluminum foil

1 tablespoon butter

1/4 cup matchstick carrots

1/4 cup dried cherry-flavored cranberries

1 cup water

2 cups homestyle herb stuffing mix

1 (8.8-ounce) package pre-cooked long grain and wild (or brown) rice

1. Remove chicken from all packaging. Wrap in aluminum foil and place in baking pan. Place in 200°F oven to keep warm.
2. Preheat large saucepan on medium-high 2–3 minutes. Combine butter, carrots, and cranberries in pan; cook 1–2 minutes or until carrots are tender.
3. Stir in water, stuffing mix, and rice; cook 1–2 minutes or until hot. Remove from heat; cover and let stand 3–5 minutes. Stir and serve.

Complete recipe:
CALORIES (per 1/4 recipe) 940kcal; FAT 51g; CHOL 240mg; SODIUM 1320mg; CARB 44g; FIBER 2g; PROTEIN 64g; VIT A 35%; VIT C 8%; CALC 4%; IRON 30%

Stuffing only:
CALORIES (per 1/4 recipe) 270kcal; FAT 7g; CHOL 10mg; SODIUM 650mg; CARB 44g; FIBER 2g; PROTEIN 5g; VIT A 30%; VIT C 2%; CALC 4%; IRON 10%

two-bean medley

1 (16-ounce) container Deli old-fashioned beans

1 (15-ounce) can black beans (drained)

1 tablespoon honey

1 tablespoon mustard

1. Combine all ingredients in microwave-safe bowl.
2. Cover and microwave on HIGH 5 minutes, stirring once, or until thoroughly heated. Stir and serve.

CALORIES (per 1/4 recipe) 280kcal; FAT 7g; CHOL 5mg; SODIUM 850mg; CARB 43g; FIBER 12g; PROTEIN 12g; VIT A 0%; VIT C 2%; CALC 10%; IRON 25%

carefree celebrations

appetizer buffet
(recipe on page 146)

standing rib roast
(recipe on page 152)

easy crowd-pleasers

When you're planning to gather family and friends at your home, you don't need to feel stress. Just reach for this cookbook, and you'll find an assortment of ideas that are sure to work well for your get-together. We believe that any of these recipes would be a surefire success for your special times. You can prepare all of them with confidence, ease, and the anticipation of lots of compliments.

NOT JUST BREAKFAST

Many times we only think of holidays as the time to fix a special breakfast meal. But maybe this weekend is all the special occasion you need. Or you can think of these as great "breakfast-for-dinner" recipes.

The French toast recipe is easy to increase for serving a crowd. The cooked slices can hold in a warm oven.

The "praline" part of this recipe happens when the moisture in the syrup (use only real maple syrup) causes the hot sugar to crystallize around the pecans. This topping would also be wonderful over pecan coffee cake or pancakes and waffles. Cook up some breakfast sausage and add some fresh cut fruit to finish this meal.

The frittata is a complete skillet meal—eggs, potatoes, salmon, veggies—all in one pan. This recipe is considered "meat" free for those that observe specific religious holiday traditions. It would also be a nice option for a wedding or baby shower, a bride's lunch, or any other type of luncheon event.

Add fresh cut fruit or a fresh salad blend along with Bakery croissants or pecan coffee cake to complete this meal.

praline french toast

salmon brunch frittata

praline french toast

4 eggs, beaten
(or 1 cup egg substitute)

1/2 cup reduced-fat milk

1 teaspoon vanilla extract

3 tablespoons butter, divided

8 (1/2-inch-thick) slices
Bakery Breakfast Bread

1/2 cup pecan halves

2 tablespoons sugar

3/4 cup maple syrup

1. Preheat oven to 200°F (for holding). Combine eggs, milk, and vanilla in shallow bowl.

2. Preheat large nonstick sauté pan on medium-high 2–3 minutes. Add 1 tablespoon of the butter; swirl to coat. Dip 4 of the bread slices, one at a time, into egg mixture, coating both sides; remove and let excess drip off, then place in pan. Cook 2–3 minutes on each side or until golden. (Place in oven, in baking pan, to keep warm until ready to serve.) Repeat with remaining 4 bread slices and 1 tablespoon butter.

3. Add remaining 1 tablespoon butter and pecans to pan. Cook 3 minutes, stirring often, or until lightly toasted and aromatic. Increase heat to high; add sugar and cook 2 more minutes, stirring continuously.

4. Remove pan from heat; stir in syrup. Serve over French toast slices.

Recipe Time: 25 minutes   Serves: 4

CALORIES (per 1/4 recipe) 648kcal; FAT 25g; CHOL 45mg; SODIUM 681mg;
CARB 95g; FIBER 4g; PROTEIN 13g; VIT A 29%; VIT C 1%; CALC 11%; IRON 27%

salmon brunch frittata

8 ounces fresh   asparagus tips
(rinsed)

1 (4-ounce) package
smoked salmon

2 tablespoons butter
(or margarine)

2 cups refrigerated homestyle
sliced potatoes

1/4 cup pre-diced red onions

1/2 teaspoon seasoned salt

6 eggs, beaten
(or 1 1/2 cups egg substitute)

1 cup shredded Swiss cheese

1/4 teaspoon dried tarragon

1. Cut asparagus into bite-size pieces. Remove skin from salmon (and discard); cut salmon into bite-size pieces. Preheat large sauté pan on medium-high 2–3 minutes.

2. Place butter in pan; swirl to coat. Add potatoes, onions, asparagus, and seasoned salt; cover and cook 5 minutes, stirring often, or until potatoes begin to brown. Add salmon; cover and cook 4–5 more minutes, stirring often, or until potatoes are tender and browned.

3. Pour eggs evenly over potato mixture and then sprinkle with cheese and tarragon (do not stir); cover and reduce to low. Cook 8–10 minutes, without stirring, or until eggs are puffy and bottom is golden. Serve.

Recipe Time: 25 Minutes   Serves: 4

CALORIES (per 1/4 recipe) 323kcal; FAT 17g; CHOL 37mg; SODIUM 986mg;
CARB 16g; FIBER 2g; PROTEIN 27g; VIT A 40%; VIT C 18%; CALC 34%; IRON 14%

PREPARATION SEQUENCE

These recipes work well together or individually.

Each recipe can be prepared, through the second step, up to 1 1/2 hours in advance.

Complete the buffet with prepared Deli platters from Publix such as sandwiches and cut cheese along with fresh-cut fruit and vegetable platters. Finish with gourmet desserts and platters from the Bakery.

Allow about an hour to complete the recipes by stuffing endive leaves, assembling beef rolls, and, just before serving, completing the crab cakes.

appetizer buffet

4 ounces premium blue cheese

3 slices prosciutto ham (about 2 ounces)

8–10 fresh basil leaves (rinsed)

36 Belgian endive leaves (2–3 heads, rinsed)

1/4 cup chopped walnuts

2 tablespoons balsamic glaze

Alternate topping: Deli Savory Tarragon Chicken Salad

blue cheese on endive

1. Crumble cheese coarsely. Stack prosciutto slices; cut into thin strips.

2. Cut basil into thin strips (2 tablespoons). Trim and discard root end of endive to separate leaves. All may be chilled until ready to prepare.

3. Arrange 36 endive leaves on serving platter. Top each with cheese, prosciutto, walnuts, and basil; drizzle lightly with glaze. Serve.

Chicken Salad on Endive: Prepare endive leaves as noted above. Top with chicken salad. Or make some with each filling.

Recipe Time: 25 minutes   Makes: 36

asian beef rolls

1 cup garlic ginger wonton strips

large zip-top bag

1 seedless cucumber (rinsed)

2 tablespoons hoisin sauce

1 teaspoon ginger spice paste

1 cup fresh bean sprouts (rinsed)

12 ounces pre-sliced Deli roast beef

3 tablespoons Asian sweet chili sauce, optional

1. Place wonton strips in zip-top bag; seal tightly and crush. Place crumbs on plate (may be paper); set aside.

2. Cut cucumber in half (reserve other half for another use); cut length in half again. Julienne by cutting each piece into thin slices; then stack slices and cut into thin, uniform matchsticks. Place in medium bowl. May be chilled until ready to prepare.

3. Stir hoisin sauce, ginger paste, and bean sprouts into cucumber strips until evenly coated. Lay beef slices flat; add 1 tablespoon of the cucumber mixture near one short end of each slice.

4. Roll beef tightly starting at short end; then carefully roll in wonton crumbs. Cut rolls into short lengths; arrange on serving platter. Top with tiny bit of chili sauce and serve.

Recipe Time: 25 minutes   Makes: about 36

crab cake bites with fruit salsa

3/4 lb Produce tropical fruit salad (fresh pineapple, strawberries, kiwi)

3–5 sprigs fresh cilantro (rinsed)

1 shallot (rinsed and peeled)

2 tablespoons honey

1 lime (rinsed)

1 head Bibb lettuce (rinsed)

6 (3-ounce) fresh premium crab cakes

2 tablespoons butter

3 tablespoons sun-dried tomato aïoli sauce (optional)

1. Cut fruit into 1/4-inch pieces; place in medium bowl. Chop cilantro finely; mince shallot finely. Stir both into fruit with honey and juice of one-half lime (1 tablespoon). Chill salsa until ready to assemble.

2. Separate 24 lettuce leaves (then chill). Divide each crab cake into four equal portions. Gently form into 24 balls (wet hands to prevent sticking); flatten to 1/2-inch thick (wash hands). Chill until ready to prepare.

3. Preheat large sauté pan on medium-high 2–3 minutes. Place 1 tablespoon of the butter in pan; swirl to coat. Gently add crab cakes and cook 4–5 minutes, without turning, or until golden.

4. Add remaining 1 tablespoon butter; turn crab cakes. Reduce to medium-low; cook 4–5 more minutes or until golden and internal temperature reaches 165°F. Use a meat thermometer to accurately ensure doneness.

5. Arrange lettuce leaves on serving platter; drizzle each with aïoli sauce. Add crab cakes; top with salsa and serve.

Recipe Time: 55 minutes   Makes: 24

PREPARATION SEQUENCE

These appetizers work well together or individually.

Here are some tips about how to organize your preparation.

About an hour before serving, prepare chicken and begin to bake. While chicken bakes, prepare dip. Complete chicken and return to oven (along with dip) to keep warm.

Prepare mini bruschettas; place in oven to keep warm.

Arrange buffet, with Deli platters you can pick up at Publix, including sandwiches, sliced meat and cheese, fresh fruit, and cut vegetables. Finish with one or more Bakery dessert platters and a colorful floral centerpiece.

Once the last recipe is in the oven, you may still have a little time to take care of any last-minute details.

deli party buffet

easy buffalo wings

2 lb Deli fried chicken wings/drummettes

1/4 cup Buffalo wing sauce (or 1/2–1 cup for hotter sauce)

1/4 cup herb garlic butter

2 teaspoons Worcestershire sauce

celery ribs and blue cheese dressing, optional

1. Preheat oven to 400°F. Arrange chicken in single layer on baking sheet. Bake 12–15 minutes or until crisp and hot.

2. Combine in microwave-safe bowl, 1/4 cup wing sauce (for mild), butter, and Worcestershire sauce. (Increase wing sauce to 1/2 cup for medium or 1 cup for hot.) Microwave on HIGH 30–60 seconds or until butter is melted. Whisk mixture until well blended.

3. If preparing ahead of time, reduce heat at end of bake time to 200°F. Drizzle sauce over chicken or reserve sauce to serve for dipping instead. Return to oven to keep warm up to 30 minutes. Serve with celery and blue cheese dressing.

   Note: Prepare additional sauce of each heat level for dipping.

Recipe Time: 25 minutes   Makes: 2 lb

2 (16-ounce) containers Deli artichoke and spinach dip

1 cup shredded Swiss cheese

8 round buttery type crackers

assorted crackers (for dipping)

hot party dip

1. Place artichoke and spinach dip in ovenproof microwave-safe dish. Microwave on HIGH 4 minutes or until dip begins to get hot.

2. Stir dip; top with cheese. Crush buttery crackers while sprinkling over top of dip. Microwave on HIGH 4 more minutes or until thoroughly heated. Let stand 5 minutes before serving (or place in 200°F oven to keep warm up to 20 minutes). Serve with assorted crackers for dipping.

Recipe Time: 15 minutes   Serves: 10 or more

2 tablespoons herb garlic butter

8 mini bagels

1/3 cup olive tapenade

2 tablespoons shredded Asiago cheese

Alternate topping: sweet onions/peppers relish, diced pepperoni

mini bruschettas

1. Place garlic butter in microwave-safe bowl; microwave on HIGH 30–40 seconds or until melted. Preheat large sauté pan on medium heat 2–3 minutes.

2. Separate bagels into two halves. Brush butter over cut side of bagels; place 8, with buttered side down, in pan. Cook 2–3 minutes until lightly browned.

3. Turn bagels and top each with 1 teaspoon tapenade; sprinkle with a bit of cheese. Cover, reduce heat to low, and cook 3–4 minutes or until heated and cheese melts. Arrange on serving tray (or on baking sheet; place in 200°F oven to keep warm up to 20 minutes). Complete remaining bagels. Serve.

Onion and Pepperoni Bruschettas: Prepare bagels as noted above. Top with 1/3 cup onions/peppers relish; sprinkle with 2 tablespoons diced pepperoni. Complete as noted.

Recipe Time: 20 minutes   Makes: 16

Sweet onions/peppers relish can usually be found in the Produce department or sometimes with Deli condiments.

PREPARATION SEQUENCE

Special occasions usually involve much more effort than everyday meals.

This is a collection of outstanding side dishes, done Simple Meals style, so you can give your attention to other details. They are designed to accompany a nice main course such as a rib roast, baked ham, or roasted turkey.

While the meat is cooking, prepare any or all of the side dishes for baking.

During the meat stand time (essential before carving), increase oven to 450°F. Bake Roasted Fall Vegetables and Asparagus Polenta Gratin for 10 minutes; then add Apple Sage Stuffing to oven (see each recipe for more details).

Complete your menu with warm dinner rolls from the Bakery, along with petite gourmet pastries.

special occasion sides

1/4 cup apple butter

1/4 cup canola oil

2 cups pre-diced fresh sweet potatoes

2 cups pre-diced fresh butternut squash

2 cups refrigerated red potato wedges

1 1/2 cups fresh baby carrots

1/2 cup pre-diced red onions

aluminum foil

1/2 teaspoon garlic salt

1/2 teaspoon seasoned pepper

roasted fall vegetables

1. Preheat oven to 450°F. Whisk apple butter and oil, in large bowl, until smooth. Stir in all vegetables until well coated.

2. Line baking sheet with foil; arrange vegetables in single layer. Sprinkle garlic salt and seasoned pepper over top. Bake 35–40 minutes, stirring occasionally, or until vegetables are tender and golden. Serve.

Recipe Time: 45 minutes   Serves: 8

1 lb ground pork sausage with sage

8 ounces trinity mix (fresh diced onions, bell peppers, celery)

1/2 cup dried berry medley (berries and raisins)

1 large Granny Smith apple (rinsed)

1 tablespoon flour

1 (14-ounce) can reduced-sodium chicken broth

1 (6-ounce) box cornbread stuffing mix

cooking spray

apple sage stuffing

1. Preheat oven to 450°F. Preheat large sauté pan on medium-high 2–3 minutes. Crumble sausage into pan (wash hands); stir in trinity mix and berries. Cook 5–7 minutes, stirring often, until meat is well browned and vegetables are tender. Meanwhile, peel apple; cut into small pieces.

2. Stir flour into sausage mixture and cook 2 minutes, stirring often, until flour is hot and well blended into mixture.

3. Stir in apple, broth, and stuffing mix until well blended. Coat 2-quart baking dish with cooking spray; add stuffing mixture. Bake 20–25 minutes or until golden and internal temperature reaches 165°F. Use a meat thermometer to accurately ensure doneness. Let stand 5 minutes before serving.

Recipe Time: 40 minutes   Serves: 8

2 tablespoons flour

1 teaspoon seasoned salt

large zip-top bag

1 lb fresh asparagus spears (rinsed)

1 (17-ounce) tube prepared polenta (plain or flavored)

2 tablespoons herb garlic butter

1 cup half-and-half

aluminum foil

1/2 cup shredded Swiss cheese

asparagus polenta gratin

1. Preheat oven to 450°F. Place flour and seasoned salt in zip-top bag; shake to mix. Cut 1 inch from tough root end of each asparagus spear and discard. To do this quickly, group half the spears together, align ends, and slice with sharp knife. Cut into 2-inch pieces; add to bag.

2. Cut tube of polenta in half (this allows wrapper to be easily removed); discard packaging. Cut into bite-size pieces and add to bag; seal tightly and gently shake to coat.

3. Place butter in small microwave-safe bowl (or into baking dish, if microwave-safe); microwave on HIGH 15–20 seconds or until butter melts. Pour into 2-quart baking dish; swirl to coat. Add asparagus mixture; then pour half-and-half evenly over mixture. Cover dish tightly with foil; bake 30 minutes.

4. Remove foil. Sprinkle cheese over top; bake 5–7 more minutes (uncovered) or until cheese melts and begins to brown. Let stand 10 minutes before serving.

Recipe Time: 1 hour   Serves: 8

shopping list

MEAT
1 (3–4 rib) standing rib roast
   (4 1/2 lb)

PRODUCE
16 ounces fresh whole
   mushrooms
8 celery ribs
2 teaspoons minced garlic

FROZEN
1/4 cup diced onions
1 (16-ounce) bag Roma blend
   vegetables (carrots,
   cauliflower, zucchini, green
   beans, and lima beans)

DAIRY
1 cup half-and-half
2 tablespoons garlic butter
1 (20-ounce) package
   refrigerated homestyle
   sliced potatoes
3/4 cup crumbled
   Gorgonzola cheese

DRY GROCERY
1 (14-ounce) can lower-
   sodium beef broth
1/4 cup French-fried onions
1 (12-ounce) jar fried peppers
   and onions
olive oil cooking spray
2 tablespoons flour
1 1/2 teaspoons coarsely
   ground pepper
2 teaspoons kosher salt

SUGGESTED ITEMS
horseradish sauce, dinner
   rolls, favorite Bakery pie

standing rib roast, gorgonzola potatoes, and vegetable sauté

MEAL TIME: *2 hours, 45 minutes*

COOKING SEQUENCE
- Prepare roast and begin to bake - 2 hours, 20 minutes
- About 25 minutes before serving roast, prepare potatoes and vegetables; serve - 25 minutes

SERVES: *8*

SHORTCUT AND TIPS
When cooking a roast, a meat thermometer is a valuable tool that can make the difference between a dinner disaster and a memorable meal.

UTENSILS AND COOKWARE
large sauté pan with lid
9 × 13-inch baking dish
microwave-safe bowl with lid
cooking spoons

meat thermometer
knife and cutting board
measuring utensils

standing rib roast

olive oil cooking spray

8 celery ribs (rinsed)

1 (3–4 rib) standing rib roast (4 1/2 lb)

2 teaspoons kosher salt

1 1/2 teaspoons coarsely ground pepper

1/4 cup frozen diced onions

2 teaspoons minced garlic

1 (14-ounce) can lower-sodium beef broth

16 ounces fresh whole mushrooms (rinsed)

1. Preheat oven to 325°F. Coat 9 × 13-inch baking dish with cooking spray.
2. Cut celery into 7-inch ribs. Lay across center of dish; place roast on top (wash hands). Sprinkle with salt, pepper, onions, and garlic.
3. Add broth and mushrooms around roast. Bake 2 1/2 hours or until internal temperature reaches 145°F (for medium-rare) to 170°F (for well-done). Use a meat thermometer to accurately ensure doneness. Let stand 10–15 minutes before slicing. Serve.

CALORIES (per 1/8 recipe) 600kcal; FAT 47g; CHOL 135mg; SODIUM 830mg; CARB 4g; FIBER 1g; PROTEIN 38g; VIT A 4%; VIT C 4%; CALC 4%; IRON 25%

gorgonzola potatoes

3/4 cup crumbled Gorgonzola cheese

1 cup half-and-half

1/2 teaspoon salt

2 tablespoons flour

2 tablespoons garlic butter

1 (20-ounce) package refrigerated homestyle sliced potatoes

1/4 cup French-fried onions

1/8 teaspoon pepper

1. Combine in microwave-safe bowl, cheese, half-and-half, salt, and flour. Add butter and microwave on HIGH 2 minutes or until hot.
2. Stir in remaining ingredients. Cover and microwave on HIGH 10 minutes, stirring once, or until potatoes are tender. Serve.

Note: For an elegant finish, place in oven-proof serving dish, top with more French-fried onions, and broil 3–5 minutes or until golden.

CALORIES (per 1/8 recipe) 170kcal; FAT 10g; CHOL 25mg; SODIUM 420mg; CARB 15g; FIBER 1g; PROTEIN 5g; VIT A 6%; VIT C 0%; CALC 8%; IRON 2%

vegetable sauté

1 (16-ounce) bag frozen Roma blend vegetables (carrots, cauliflower, zucchini, green beans, and lima beans)

1 (12-ounce) jar fried peppers and onions

1/2 teaspoon salt

1/8 teaspoon pepper

1. Preheat large sauté pan on medium-high 2–3 minutes. Place all ingredients in pan. Cook 2–3 minutes, stirring occasionally, until blended.
2. Reduce heat to medium-low; cover and cook 5–7 minutes, stirring occasionally, or until tender. Serve.

CALORIES (per 1/8 recipe) 60kcal; FAT 2g; CHOL 0mg; SODIUM 410mg; CARB 8g; FIBER 3g; PROTEIN 1g; VIT A 20%; VIT C 110%; CALC 2%; IRON 2%

You can choose your family's favorite mix of frozen vegetables for the Vegetable Sauté recipe.

shopping list

MEAT

1 semi-boneless fully cooked
   ham half (6–8 lb)

PRODUCE

16 ounces baby carrots
8 ounces sugar snap peas

FROZEN

16 ounces cauliflower florets

DAIRY

3 tablespoons butter

DRY GROCERY

1 (16-ounce) can whole
   cranberry sauce
1/4 cup roasted red peppers
2 tablespoons
   balsamic vinegar
2 tablespoons brown sugar
3/4 teaspoon garlic salt
1/2 teaspoon seasoned salt
1/4 teaspoon seasoned
   pepper blend
aluminum foil
1/4 cup guava jelly
1/2 cup dried tropical fruit
   bits (mango, pineapple,
   papaya)
1/4 cup cream sherry

SUGGESTED ITEMS

green beans, mashed
   potatoes, dinner rolls,
   pecan pie

ham with chutney, red pepper cauliflower, and carrot sugar snaps

MEAL TIME: *about 2 1/2 hours*

COOKING SEQUENCE

- Prepare ham and bake - 2 hours or more
- While ham stands, begin chutney, begin cauliflower, and
  then begin carrots - 5 minutes
- Complete chutney, then carrots, and then cauliflower;
  serve - 20 minutes

SERVES: 6 *(with leftovers)*

SHORTCUT AND TIPS

Wrapping the ham in foil before heating will help ensure that it stays
moist and flavorful.

UTENSILS AND COOKWARE

shallow baking pan
2 medium saucepans (1 with lid)
steamer insert
microwave-safe bowl with lid

cooking spoons
meat thermometer
knife and cutting board
measuring utensils

ham with chutney

1 semi-boneless fully cooked ham half (6–8 lb)

aluminum foil

1 (16-ounce) can whole cranberry sauce

1/2 cup dried tropical fruit bits (mango, pineapple, papaya)

1/4 cup cream sherry

2 tablespoons brown sugar

2 tablespoons balsamic vinegar

1. Preheat oven to 325°F. Remove all packaging and wrap ham in foil; place in shallow baking pan. Bake about 20 minutes per pound or just until internal temperature at center of ham is at least 130°F. Use a meat thermometer to accurately ensure doneness. Remove ham from oven and let stand 10–20 minutes before slicing (temperature will rise during stand time to 140°F).

2. While ham stands, combine remaining ingredients in medium saucepan until blended; bring to boil on medium-high. Boil chutney 2 minutes.

3. Reduce heat to low; cook 10–12 minutes, stirring occasionally, or until sauce thickens and fruit softens. Slice ham and serve with chutney. (Ham makes 12–16 servings; chutney makes 2 cups.)

CALORIES (per 1/14 ham [7 lb] and 1/10 sauce) 450kcal; FAT 26g; CHOL 100mg; SODIUM 1540mg; CARB 26g; FIBER 1g; PROTEIN 24g; VIT A 2%; VIT C 0%; CALC 0%; IRON 8%

red pepper cauliflower

1–1 1/2 cups water

16 ounces frozen cauliflower florets

1/4 cup roasted red peppers

1 tablespoon butter

3/4 teaspoon garlic salt

1/4 teaspoon seasoned pepper blend

1. Place steamer insert and water (about 1/2-inch deep, but below bottom of insert) in medium saucepan. Add cauliflower; cover and bring to boil on high.

2. Steam 4–5 minutes or until desired doneness. Meanwhile, cut peppers into thin strips.

3. Carefully remove steamer basket with cauliflower from saucepan (will be very HOT); discard water. Place all ingredients in same saucepan. Stir until butter melts (over residual heat only). Serve.

CALORIES (per 1/6 recipe) 40kcal; FAT 2g; CHOL 5mg; SODIUM 170mg; CARB 4g; FIBER 7g; PROTEIN 2g; VIT A 8%; VIT C 70%; CALC 2%; IRON 2%

carrot sugar snaps

16 ounces baby carrots

2 tablespoons butter

1/2 teaspoon seasoned salt

8 ounces fresh sugar snap peas (rinsed)

1/4 cup guava jelly

1. Place carrots, butter, and seasoned salt in microwave-safe bowl. Cover and microwave on HIGH 4 minutes or until carrots begin to soften. Meanwhile, snip ends off snap peas, if needed.

2. Stir in snap peas; cover and microwave on HIGH 4 more minutes or until desired tenderness. Stir in jelly and serve.

CALORIES (per 1/6 recipe) 170kcal; FAT 6g; CHOL 15mg; SODIUM 330mg; CARB 27g; FIBER 3g; PROTEIN 2g; VIT A 330%; VIT C 35%; CALC 8%; IRON 10%

shopping list

MEAT

1 whole chicken
   (about 3 1/2 lb)

PRODUCE

3 large sweet potatoes
1 lemon
2–4 sprigs fresh rosemary

FROZEN

14 ounces whole green beans

DAIRY

2 tablespoons garlic butter
1 tablespoon butter

DRY GROCERY

1/4 cup light mayonnaise
1 tablespoon cinnamon-sugar
1 tablespoon minced onions
1 teaspoon seasoned salt

SUGGESTED ITEMS

stuffing (from mix), gravy,
   strawberry dessert

rosemary chicken, stovetop sweet potatoes, and seasoned beans

MEAL TIME: *1 hour, 35 minutes*

COOKING SEQUENCE

- Prepare chicken and bake about 50 minutes - 1 hour, 5 minutes
- Prepare sweet potatoes and begin to boil - 10 minutes
- During chicken stand time, prepare beans; carve chicken and serve - 20 minutes

SERVES: 6

SHORTCUT AND TIPS

The mayonnaise acts as a "self-basting" ingredient. Slowly basting the chicken as it cooks draws the rosemary flavor deep into the meat.

UTENSILS AND COOKWARE

baking dish (or roasting pan)   cooking spoons
large saucepan with lid   meat thermometer
large sauté pan with lid   knife and cutting board
colander, kitchen shears   measuring utensils

rosemary chicken

1 whole chicken (about 3 1/2 lb)

1 teaspoon seasoned salt

2–4 sprigs fresh rosemary (rinsed)

1 lemon (rinsed)

1/4 cup light mayonnaise

1 tablespoon minced onions

1. Preheat oven to 375°F. Remove giblets from chicken (reserve for later use or discard). Pat chicken dry. Place chicken in baking dish (or roasting pan). Season inside and outside of chicken with seasoned salt (wash hands).

2. Snip rosemary, leaves only, using kitchen shears; sprinkle one-half of the rosemary inside chicken. Cut lemon in half; place both halves inside chicken.

3. Coat outside of chicken with mayonnaise (wash hands). Sprinkle with remaining one-half of rosemary and onions. Bake 1 hour and 20 minutes, or until internal temperature of chicken reaches 165°F. Use a meat thermometer to accurately ensure doneness. Let chicken stand 5–10 minutes before carving. Serve.

CALORIES (per 1/6 recipe) 410kcal; FAT 30g; CHOL 135mg; SODIUM 440mg; CARB 1g; FIBER 0g; PROTEIN 33g; VIT A 6%; VIT C 6%; CALC 2%; IRON 8%

stovetop sweet potatoes

3 large sweet potatoes (rinsed)

2 cups water

1 tablespoon butter

1/4 teaspoon salt

1 tablespoon cinnamon-sugar

1. Peel sweet potatoes. Slice into quarters lengthwise, then cut into 1-inch chunks. Place in large sauté pan with water. Cover and bring to boil on high.

2. Reduce heat to medium-high; boil 12–15 minutes, stirring occasionally, or until tender when pierced with a fork.

3. Drain potatoes; return to pan. Stir in remaining ingredients and serve.

CALORIES (per 1/6 recipe) 80kcal; FAT 2g; CHOL 5mg; SODIUM 150mg; CARB 15g; FIBER 2g; PROTEIN 1g; VIT A 190%; VIT C 2%; CALC 2%; IRON 2%

seasoned beans

14 ounces frozen whole green beans

2 tablespoons garlic butter

1/4 teaspoon salt

1/8 teaspoon pepper

1. Place beans in microwave-safe bowl. Cover and microwave on HIGH 8 minutes, stirring once, or until desired tenderness.

2. Drain beans; stir in remaining ingredients. Serve.

CALORIES (per 1/6 recipe) 50kcal; FAT 4g; CHOL 5mg; SODIUM 135mg; CARB 4g; FIBER 2g; PROTEIN 1g; VIT A 10%; VIT C 10%; CALC 2%; IRON 2%

shopping list

MEAT

1 boneless pork roast
   (about 1 1/2 lb)

PRODUCE

1 (24-ounce) jar tropical fruit
   in light syrup (pineapple
   and papaya)
1 Granny Smith apple
1 lemon (for juice)
2 tablespoons pine nuts

DAIRY

2 prepared pie crusts
1 tablespoon butter

DRY GROCERY

1 (21-ounce) can blueberry
   (or peach) pie filling
1/2 cup reduced-sodium
   chicken broth
2 tablespoons olive oil
1/4 cup molasses
1 teaspoon turbinado
   (raw) sugar
1 tablespoon cornstarch
1/2 teaspoon ground
   cinnamon
1/4 teaspoon ground allspice
nonstick aluminum foil

SUGGESTED ITEMS

rice, fresh salad blend,
   dinner rolls

pork roast with tropical fruit sauce and blueberry pouch pie

MEAL TIME: *50 minutes*

COOKING SEQUENCE

• Prepare pork and begin to bake - 10 minutes
• Prepare pies and begin to bake (in same oven) - 15 minutes
• Prepare fruit sauce and serve - 25 minutes

SERVES: *4*

SHORTCUT AND TIPS

Replace the blueberry pie filling and apples with your favorite
combination of pie filling and fresh fruit.

UTENSILS AND COOKWARE

2 baking sheets
wire cooling rack
large sauté pan
medium saucepan
small microwave-safe bowl

mixing bowls, cooking spoons
basting brush, meat
   thermometer
tongs, knife, and cutting board
measuring utensils

1 boneless pork roast
(about 1 1/2 lb)

3/4 teaspoon salt, divided

3/4 teaspoon pepper, divided

2 tablespoons olive oil

1 (24-ounce) jar tropical fruit in
light syrup (pineapple and
papaya), undrained

1/2 cup reduced-sodium
chicken broth

1/4 cup molasses

2 tablespoons pine nuts

1/2 teaspoon ground cinnamon

1 tablespoon cornstarch

1/4 cup water

pork roast with tropical fruit sauce

1. Preheat oven to 400°F (lower one rack for pork; raise one rack for pies to bake above pork). Season pork with 1/2 teaspoon each of the salt and pepper; set aside. Preheat large sauté pan on medium-high 3–4 minutes.

2. Place oil in pan; swirl to coat. Add pork to pan (wash hands); cook 5 minutes, turning often, or until well browned.

3. Transfer pork to a foil-lined baking sheet (for ease in cleanup). Bake 35–40 minutes or until internal temperature reaches 160°F (for medium). Use a meat thermometer to accurately ensure doneness. Let meat rest 5 minutes before slicing.

4. During last 15 minutes of bake time, combine in medium saucepan, fruit (with syrup), broth, molasses, pine nuts, cinnamon, and remaining 1/4 teaspoon each salt and pepper. Bring to a boil on medium heat.

5. Combine cornstarch and water in small bowl until well blended. Add to sauce and return to boiling; cook 2–3 minutes, stirring often, or until sauce begins to thicken. Slice pork and top with fruit sauce; serve.

CALORIES (per 1/4 recipe) 630kcal; FAT 34g; CHOL 105mg; SODIUM 550mg; CARB 47g; FIBER 2g; PROTEIN 35g; VIT A 6%; VIT C 140%; CALC 6%; IRON 20%

2 prepared pie crusts

1 Granny Smith apple (rinsed)

1 lemon (for juice, rinsed)

1 (21-ounce) can blueberry
(or peach) pie filling

1/4 teaspoon ground allspice

nonstick aluminum foil

1 tablespoon butter

1 teaspoon turbinado (raw) sugar

blueberry pouch pie

1. Preheat oven to 400°F. Remove pie crusts from package and let stand 4–5 minutes. Peel and core apple; cut (or dice) into small pieces and place in medium bowl. Squeeze juice of lemon over apple; stir until evenly coated. Stir in pie filling and allspice until well blended.

2. Place 2 (10 × 12-inch) nonstick foil sheets on work surface. Unroll crusts over foil sheets. Pour half of filling into center of each pie crust. Fold edge of pie crust toward center, over filling. Work clockwise around edge of pie crust, overlapping folds, and leaving about 2–3 inches open in center. Repeat with second pie. Gently transfer pies (on foil) to baking sheet.

3. Place butter in small microwave-safe bowl; microwave 20–30 seconds or until butter melts. Brush crusts with butter; sprinkle with sugar. Bake pies 25–30 minutes or until tops are golden.

4. Transfer pies (on foil) to wire cooling rack. Let stand 15 minutes before serving. (Makes 12 servings.)

CALORIES (per 1/12 recipe) 270kcal; FAT 10g; CHOL 10mg; SODIUM 150mg; CARB 41g; FIBER 2g; PROTEIN 2g; VIT A 0%; VIT C 4%; CALC 2%; IRON 2%

shopping list

MEAT

2 pork tenderloins
  (about 2 lb)

PRODUCE

2 fresh garlic cloves
1 teaspoon finely
  chopped ginger

DAIRY

2 tablespoons butter

DRY GROCERY

1 (10.5-ounce) can
  condensed beef consommé
1 (10.5-ounce) can
  condensed French
  onion soup
1/2 cup lite soy sauce
1 cup long grain rice
1 (2.6-ounce) jar
  sesame seeds
2 tablespoons minced onions
3 tablespoons sugar
cooking spray
large zip-top bag

SUGGESTED ITEMS

Deli coleslaw, sugar snap
  peas, fresh pineapple,
  almond creme cake

korean pork strips with french onion rice

MEAL TIME: *55 minutes*

COOKING SEQUENCE

- Preheat oven, prepare rice, and begin to bake - 10 minutes
- Prepare pork, place in oven with rice, and continue baking; serve - 45 minutes

SERVES: 6

SHORTCUT AND TIPS

This rice recipe can be doubled for large families or parties. Use a 9 × 13-inch baking dish.

UTENSILS AND COOKWARE

9 × 13-inch baking dish   meat thermometer
2-quart baking dish with lid   knife and cutting board
garlic press, tongs   measuring utensils
cooking spoon

korean pork strips

2 fresh garlic cloves

large zip-top bag

1 (2.6-ounce) jar sesame seeds

1/2 cup lite soy sauce

3 tablespoons sugar

2 tablespoons minced onions

1 teaspoon finely chopped ginger

2 pork tenderloins (about 2 lb)

cooking spray

1. Preheat oven to 400°F. Crush garlic cloves, using garlic press, into large zip-top bag. Use knife to scrape bottom of garlic press.
2. Add remaining ingredients (except pork). Shake bag to mix.
3. Slice pork in half lengthwise and add to marinade (wash hands). Knead bag to coat pork well; let stand 5 minutes. (For additional flavor, pork can marinate 2–3 hours in refrigerator before cooking.)
4. Coat 9 × 13-inch baking dish with cooking spray. Place tenderloins in pan; top with remaining marinade. Bake 25–30 minutes or until internal temperature of pork reaches 160°F (for medium). Use a meat thermometer to accurately ensure doneness.
5. Let pork stand 5 minutes before slicing. Use a clean knife and cutting board to cut pork into thin slices and serve.

CALORIES (per 1/6 recipe) 300kcal; FAT 11g; CHOL 100mg; SODIUM 880mg; CARB 12g; FIBER 2g; PROTEIN 36g; VIT A 0%; VIT C 8%; CALC 15%; IRON 20%

french onion rice

1 cup long grain rice

1 (10.5-ounce) can condensed beef consommé

1 (10.5-ounce) can condensed French onion soup

2 tablespoons butter

1. Preheat oven to 400°F. Place rice in 2-quart baking dish. Stir in beef consommé and French onion soup.
2. Cut butter into thin slices and arrange evenly over top of rice. Cover and bake 40–45 minutes or until rice has completely absorbed liquid. Let stand 5 minutes before serving.

CALORIES (per 1/6 recipe) 180kcal; FAT 4.5g; CHOL 10mg; SODIUM 660mg; CARB 28g; FIBER 1g; PROTEIN 5g; VIT A 2%; VIT C 0%; CALC 2%; IRON 8%

Lining the baking dishes with nonstick foil would make cleanup simple and quick. The easiest way to line a baking dish with foil is to turn the dish UPSIDE DOWN and wrap the foil around the outside of the dish. Then simply slip the "formed" foil off the dish, turn the dish over, and drop the perfect-fitting foil inside the dish.

shopping list

SEAFOOD

3/4 lb peeled/deveined shrimp
3/4 lb bay scallops

PRODUCE

4 ounces pre-sliced baby
  portabella mushrooms
1–2 green onions
4–5 sprigs fresh Italian parsley
1 lemon (for juice)

FROZEN

1 (10-ounce) package puff
  pastry shells
1 (16-ounce) bag green peas

DAIRY

2 tablespoons garlic butter

DRY GROCERY

1/2 cup Alfredo sauce
1 tablespoon basil pesto
1/2 teaspoon seasoned salt
1 tablespoon flour

SUGGESTED ITEMS

quick-cooking rice blend,
  creme cake

seafood in pastry with green peas

MEAL TIME: *40 minutes*

COOKING SEQUENCE

- Preheat oven and begin to bake pastry shells - 10 minutes
- Continue seafood through step 3 - 15 minutes
- Prepare peas; complete seafood and serve - 15 minutes

SERVES: *4*

SHORTCUT AND TIPS

Want a great meal in less time? Serve the seafood mixture tossed with cooked angel hair pasta.

UTENSILS AND COOKWARE

large sauté pan, baking sheet   knife and cutting board
microwave-safe bowl with lid   measuring utensils
cooking spoons

1 (10-ounce) package frozen puff pastry shells

4–5 sprigs fresh Italian parsley

1–2 green onions

1 lemon (for juice)

4 ounces pre-sliced baby portabella mushrooms

1 tablespoon garlic butter

3/4 lb peeled/deveined shrimp (thawed, if needed)

3/4 lb bay scallops (thawed, if needed)

1 tablespoon basil pesto

1 tablespoon flour

1/2 cup Alfredo sauce

seafood in pastry

1. Preheat oven to 400°F. Place pastry shells (top side up) on baking sheet. Bake shells 20–25 minutes or until golden and puffed.

2. Meanwhile, rinse parsley, onions, lemon, and mushrooms. Chop parsley finely (2 tablespoons); chop green onions finely. Cut lemon in half; set all aside.

3. Preheat large sauté pan on medium-high 2–3 minutes. Place butter in pan; swirl to coat. Add mushrooms, shrimp, scallops, and pesto. Cook 4–5 minutes, stirring occasionally, or until mushrooms are tender and both shrimp and scallops are opaque.

4. Stir in flour, Alfredo sauce, juice of one-half lemon, parsley, and onions. Cook 1–2 minutes, stirring occasionally, or until slightly thickened.

5. Place pastry shells on serving plates. Remove tops, using a fork, and hollow out center of shells; discard the extra pastry. Fill shells with seafood mixture and serve. (Makes 6 servings.)

CALORIES (per 1/6 recipe) 380kcal; FAT 21g; CHOL 120mg; SODIUM 590mg; CARB 22g; FIBER 1g; PROTEIN 27g; VIT A 8%; VIT C 10%; CALC 6%; IRON 20%

1 (16-ounce) bag frozen green peas

1 tablespoon garlic butter

1/2 teaspoon seasoned salt

green peas

1. Place peas in microwave-safe bowl. Cover and microwave on HIGH 6–8 minutes, stirring once, or until peas are tender.

2. Drain peas. Stir in butter and seasoned salt; serve.

CALORIES (per 1/4 recipe) 110kcal; FAT 3g; CHOL 5mg; SODIUM 340mg; CARB 16g; FIBER 5g; PROTEIN 6g; VIT A 50%; VIT C 35%; CALC 2%; IRON 10%

shopping list

MEAT

1 1/2 lb grilling steaks
(such as ribeye, top sirloin,
or strip)

SEAFOOD

4 (5-ct) shrimp-on-a-skewer

PRODUCE

8–10 sprigs fresh thyme
1 tablespoon pre-sliced
green onions

DAIRY

1 (24-ounce) package
refrigerated mashed
potatoes
1/4 cup shredded
Cheddar cheese
1/4 cup sour cream

DRY GROCERY

1 tablespoon cooked
bacon pieces
2 teaspoons seasoned
pepper blend
2 tablespoons dried
parsley flakes
1 1/2 teaspoons garlic salt
olive oil cooking spray

SUGGESTED ITEMS

fresh salad blend, dinner rolls,
cheesecake

herb-rubbed surf and turf with loaded mashed potatoes

MEAL TIME: *20 minutes*

COOKING SEQUENCE

- Preheat grill
- Prepare steak and shrimp; begin to grill - 10 minutes
- Prepare potatoes and complete grilling; serve - 10 minutes

SERVES: *4*

SHORTCUT AND TIPS

For more intense flavor, let just the steaks marinate in refrigerator
overnight. Be sure to divide herb mixture, so shrimp can be coated just
before grilling.

UTENSILS AND COOKWARE

grill, grilling tongs
food processor
  (or food chopper)
microwave-safe bowl with lid

cooking spoon
meat thermometer
knife and cutting board
measuring utensils

8–10 sprigs fresh thyme (rinsed)

2 tablespoons dried parsley flakes

2 teaspoons seasoned
pepper blend

1 1/2 teaspoons garlic salt

1 1/2 lb grilling steaks (such as
ribeye, top sirloin, or strip)

4 (5-ct) shrimp-on-a-skewer
(thawed, if needed)

olive oil cooking spray

herb-rubbed surf and turf

1. Preheat grill. Process thyme (leaves only), parsley, pepper blend, and garlic salt in food processor (or food chopper) 10–15 seconds or until coarsely chopped and well mixed. Place mixture on plate.

2. Cut steaks into 4 portions. Coat steaks and shrimp skewers by pressing into herb rub, then turn and coat other side; shake gently to remove excess rub. Discard remaining rub that has been in contact with raw meat; wash hands.

3. Coat steaks and shrimp with cooking spray. Place steak (only) on grill (wash hands); grill 5 minutes. Turn steaks, place shrimp on grill. Cook 2 minutes; turn shrimp and cook 1–3 minutes or until internal temperature of steak (for medium-rare) and shrimp reaches 145°F. Use a meat thermometer to accurately ensure doneness. (Grills vary widely; adjust time as needed.) Serve.

CALORIES (per 1/4 recipe) 310kcal; FAT 14g; CHOL 150mg; SODIUM 510mg; CARB 3g; FIBER 0g; PROTEIN 41g; VIT A 4%; VIT C 2%; CALC 4%; IRON 25%

1 (24-ounce) package refrigerated
mashed potatoes

1/4 cup shredded Cheddar cheese

1/4 cup sour cream

1 tablespoon cooked bacon pieces

1 tablespoon pre-sliced
green onions

loaded mashed potatoes

1. Combine all ingredients in microwave-safe bowl.

2. Cover and microwave on HIGH 2 minutes; stir and heat 2–3 more minutes or until hot. Stir before serving.

CALORIES (per 1/4 recipe) 270kcal; FAT 17g; CHOL 45mg; SODIUM 700mg; CARB 21g; FIBER 1g; PROTEIN 5g; VIT A 15%; VIT C 0%; CALC 10%; IRON 2%

shopping list

MEAT

3 boneless, skinless
   chicken breasts (1 1/2 lb)

PRODUCE

2 medium tomatoes
8 ounces three-color cole
   slaw mix
1 pint strawberries
   (2 1/2 cups)

FROZEN

1 (11.5-ounce) pecan
   coffee cake
8 ounces light
   whipped topping

DAIRY

2 tablespoons butter
1/4 cup French vanilla
   nondairy creamer
1 1/4 cups shredded Cheddar-
   Jack cheese
3/4 cup shredded tomato/
   basil mozzarella cheese

DRY GROCERY

6 tablespoons sun-dried
   tomato pesto
2 tablespoons vegetable oil
3/4 cup cole slaw dressing
3/4 cup plain bread crumbs

SUGGESTED ITEMS

rice pilaf, garlic bread

tomato pesto chicken, cole slaw crisp, and strawberry-pecan fool

MEAL TIME: *60 minutes*

COOKING SEQUENCE

- Preheat oven; prepare dessert through step 2 - 10 minutes
- Prepare cole slaw recipe and begin to bake - 15 minutes
- Prepare chicken through step 5; complete cole slaw recipe - 25 minutes
- While chicken cooks, complete dessert; serve - 10 minutes

SERVES: *4*

SHORTCUT AND TIPS

The coffee cake in the dessert recipe does not need to be thawed; it is easier to cut when still partially frozen.

UTENSILS AND COOKWARE

large sauté pan with lid
2-quart baking dish
mixing bowls
dessert bowl, whisk

turning spatula
cooking spoon, meat thermometer
knife and cutting board
measuring utensils

tomato pesto chicken

2 medium tomatoes (rinsed)

3 boneless, skinless chicken breasts (1 1/2 lb)

1/2 teaspoon salt

1/4 teaspoon pepper

2 tablespoons vegetable oil

6 tablespoons sun-dried tomato pesto

3/4 cup shredded tomato/basil mozzarella cheese

1. Cut six 1/4-inch-thick slices from tomatoes; set aside.
2. Trim excess fat from chicken; cut chicken into six equal pieces (squares). Season with salt and pepper (wash hands). Preheat large sauté pan on medium-high 2–3 minutes.
3. Place oil in pan; swirl to coat. Place chicken in pan (wash hands); cook 4–5 minutes on each side, turning only once, or until golden.
4. Reduce heat to medium-low. Top each with 1 tablespoon of the pesto, 1 tomato slice, and then 2 tablespoons of the cheese.
5. Cover and cook 10–12 minutes or until cheese melts and internal temperature of chicken reaches 165°F. Use a meat thermometer to accurately ensure doneness. Serve.

CALORIES (per 1/4 recipe) 340kcal; FAT 14g; CHOL 110mg; SODIUM 750mg; CARB 7g; FIBER 1g; PROTEIN 45g; VIT A 20%; VIT C 20%; CALC 15%; IRON 10%

cole slaw crisp

2 tablespoons butter

8 ounces three-color cole slaw mix

3/4 cup cole slaw dressing

1 1/4 cups shredded Cheddar-Jack cheese, divided

1/4 teaspoon salt

1/4 teaspoon pepper

3/4 cup plain bread crumbs

1. Preheat oven to 400°F. Cut butter into small pieces while placing in medium bowl; set aside to soften.
2. Combine in a large bowl, cole slaw mix, dressing, 1 cup of the cheese, salt, and pepper; mix well until blended. Spoon mixture evenly into 2-quart baking dish.
3. Stir bread crumbs and remaining 1/4 cup cheese into softened butter; mix with fingertips until mixture is blended and crumbly. Spread evenly over cole slaw mixture. Bake 15–20 minutes or until golden and bubbly around edges. Let stand 5 minutes; serve warm. (Makes 6 servings.)

CALORIES (per 1/6 recipe) 290kcal; FAT 22g; CHOL 45mg; SODIUM 580mg; CARB 17g; FIBER 1g; PROTEIN 8g; VIT A 20%; VIT C 20%; CALC 20%; IRON 4%

strawberry-pecan fool

8 ounces frozen light whipped topping

1/4 cup French vanilla nondairy creamer

1 (11.5-ounce) frozen pecan coffee cake

1 pint strawberries (2 1/2 cups)

1. Place topping and creamer in medium bowl. Cut cake into 1-inch cubes. Rinse berries, remove stems, and slice thinly (reserving 1 berry for garnish). Set all aside.
2. Whisk topping and creamer until smooth.
3. Place half of the cake cubes in dessert bowl. Layer with half of the berries and then half of the topping mixture (smooth with back of spoon). Repeat layers. Garnish with last berry. Chill until ready to serve. (Makes 6 servings.)

CALORIES (per 1/6 recipe) 320kcal; FAT 16g; CHOL 15mg; SODIUM 220mg; CARB 42g; FIBER 2g; PROTEIN 3g; VIT A 0%; VIT C 60%; CALC 0%; IRON 8%

healthier options

sautéed fish and
tropical salsa
(recipe on page 86)

balsamic chicken
and vegetables
(recipe on page 64)

HEALTHIER OPTIONS

general overview

The overwhelming majority of us who still cook on a regular basis do so for good reasons. Cooking is much more economical than eating out. Just as important is the ability to control both the freshness and the nutritional value of your meals. We believe that you can have a well-balanced diet by combining moderation with a wide variety of foods. This section contains useful information about making healthier choices to improve the nutritional value of your meals as well as how to meet some types of dietary restrictions or concerns that your family may have. This is one of the exciting aspects of Apron's Simple Meals—you get to decide what goes into your recipes and can adjust the ingredients to meet your family's specific needs.

Nutritional analysis is not an exact science, but is rather a guideline for you to use on your quest for a balanced diet. Nutritional values can vary based on the amount, the brand, or even the freshness of the ingredient used. Our nutritional values are derived from many sources—including the United States Department of Agriculture tables, computer data banks, product labeling, and various Web sites—and are more complete than average recipes.

We also have worked very hard to balance our menus just as mom would, providing you with a satisfying meal containing a variety of proteins, starches, and vegetables. We invite you to read on to learn more about dietary changes that you can make to fit your lifestyle.

FAT

understanding calories and fat grams

Fat is an essential part of our diet. It is important for brain and nerve tissue development. The USDA allows for 30% of our daily calories to come from fat. So, for a 2000-calorie-a-day diet, that comes out to 600 calories and approximately 67 fat grams. If you're like most of our customers, dividing your calories between 3 meals a day, this would equate to 22 fat grams at every meal. The allowance is higher for men and teenagers. We have over 30 meals in this cookbook that come close to or are less than this figure (per meal serving) already, but if you really want to reduce more fat grams read on.

reducing fat from butter and oils

As we stated in our staples and standbys section, butter is our flavor of choice in many recipes, and we use it often. We also use a small amount of either canola or olive oil to promote browning when sautéing. In terms of calories and fat grams, all fats are the same. The main difference is that butter contains saturated fat and cholesterol. If you want to reduce the total fat, saturated fat, and cholesterol, substitute a smaller amount of butter or oil or use a cooking spray. Soft tub margarine may also be used instead of butter, but it may not produce the same quality product in all recipes.

reducing fat from dairy products

Cheese is one way to add calcium to your diet and punch up the flavor as well. But if you really want to cut fat calories, reduce the cheese. Most cheeses are high in fat, with Cheddar and Swiss coming in at 7 to 9 fat grams per 1/4 cup. Sour cream is even higher at 12 grams per 1/4 cup. You can substitute a lower-fat variety to help reduce those fat grams, understanding that some of these may not melt quite the same or be as creamy.

When choosing milk or cream, we usually call for the lowest fat variety that will produce the best quality recipe. Most of the time, you can choose lower-fat options, just remembering that some choices may not have the same flavor and thickening properties. Instead of whole milk, use reduced-fat milk or undiluted evaporated milk for sauces, soups, and gravies.

You will find that our recipes give the option of using egg substitute for whole eggs; this is one way to lower the cholesterol content in recipes.

reducing fat naturally

You can lower your fat calories by choosing meals that are naturally lower in fat, such as recipes with a high vegetable or grain content, that are centered around skinless poultry or seafood, and that do not contain a large amount of added butter, cream, or oil. Balance your diet by choosing leaner cuts of meat and poultry, trimmed of fat and skin, instead of higher-fat cuts of beef or pork. You can also choose to follow the USDA guidelines for portion size of proteins. Many of our recipes that indicate four servings actually have six ounces of protein in each serving. This is based on our research about what most people are actually eating and not necessarily based on the USDA recommendation. You may choose to make four smaller servings, saving a couple for the next day's lunch, and then increase the amount of vegetables or grains served on the side to complete your meal.

SODIUM

understanding sodium

Sodium is also an essential nutrient in keeping our bodies healthy, necessary for the operation of the nervous system and for muscle control. The USDA allows for 2300 milligrams of sodium per day for most population groups (approximately one teaspoon), but only 1500 milligrams a day for African Americans, middle-aged and older adults, or those with high blood pressure. Americans typically consume much more sodium than that each day. In fact, according to the Salt Institute, most Americans consume about 3500 milligrams each day. The American Dietetic Association places consumption as high as 7,000 to 14,000 milligrams every day.

reducing sodium from processed foods

Unfortunately, along with the convenience and saving of time that many processed foods have to offer, they are also usually high in sodium. To minimize sodium from these products here are some tips:

- Only use a portion of the seasoning flavor packet in rice or couscous mixes, which is mostly sodium;

- Substitute the low- or lower-sodium variety for ingredients such as broths, canned vegetables, and condiments;

- Use no-salt-added butter in recipes, which is what many professional chefs prefer to use;

- Avoid regular versions of cured products, such as ham and bacon, or reduce the amount that you use;

- Look for salt-free versions of seasoning blends, such as salt-free steak or poultry seasoning.

CARBOHYDRATES

understanding carbohydrates

Carbohydrates are also an essential nutrient, providing our bodies with energy; therefore it is unhealthy to try and completely eliminate them from our diet. Like fats, they come in many forms, with some forms healthier than others. For a balanced diet, along with weight management, it is important that the bulk of carbohydrates come from whole grains, fruits, and vegetables, and that the daily amount falls within a range of 45 to 65 percent of total calories. These forms of carbohydrates, generally fiber-rich, provide our bodies with the nutrients they need without a lot of added calories or fat. Other types of carbohydrates, such as desserts and sugar-sweetened beverages, add extra calories without many nutrients. Once again, moderation is the key. All forms of carbohydrates can be enjoyed as long as they are in the right balance.

reducing carbohydrates

To help reduce the amount of added sugars in your family's diet, and to increase the intake of whole grains, fruits, and vegetables, we offer the following suggestions:

- Substitute fresh fruit, or canned fruit packed in its own juice, for regular desserts or dessert recipes;

- Choose low-calorie or diet beverages, or sweeten your beverages with a sugar substitute instead of sugar;

- Replace the sugar, in some dessert recipes, with a sugar substitute (following the manufacturer's substitution guidelines);

- Choose whole-grain varieties of rice and pasta, instead of regular ones, allowing for any extra water or cook time that may be needed.

SPECIAL NOTES

As always, the information we have provided is not meant to replace that of your doctor or medical provider. These are just general dietary guidelines that may help you make healthier choices. Anyone with dietary or health problems, or whose diets require close monitoring, should not rely solely on the nutritional information provided.

Take the time to learn more about appropriate portion sizes, about lifestyle and dietary changes that may help to improve the quality of your life, and about general food safety guidelines. For additional information on healthier dietary options, you can go on line and visit www.MyPyramid.gov, www.health.gov/DietaryGuidelines, and www.eatright.org.